Robert Lansdorp's Building A Champion

Copyright
All Rights Reserved
2025

ISBN:978-1-942597-14-8

In Loving Memory Of

Robert Herman Lansdorp

November 12, 1938 -
September 16, 2024

Foreword

This is a tricky little fragmented book. Similar to Bruce Lee's The Tao of Jeet Kune Do, also not a completed work by its original author. Robert's successes rivaled Bruce Lee, and their approach to training was similar. In discussing helping Robert publish his book, the process started well and went quickly. Robert handed over everything that he had written or was written about him. But, his high level of perfectionism took over, the work was ultimately produced by someone else. He did not hold the same level of perfectionism in his own production of content, which creates a conflict for those who would have enjoyed a more polished work. One of the endearing, but necessary spects of editing the book was removing expletives from the text, although some were left in, so that you can capture the real flavor of Robert's interactions. The content was created over about a 10 year period, explaining some of the player references. AI was used to compile and rewrite a collection of biographical information, condensing it into one coherent biographical chapter.

Some chapters were taken from articles written about Robert, written by him, and others are samples of interview questions. Robert rarely sat for an interview, but in the editor's case, it was a full day of filming. The editor does not defend the off color things he has said, nor some of his dubious actions. If you can forgive Robert's infrequent misdeeds, and take the product of his life as a whole, you will be more blessed for it. More often than not, it was Coach Lansdorp who said and did things that others were afraid to say or do, and he was very influential because of his bravery in that regard to truth telling.

When Robert saw the first draft of the edit of this compiled work, with some more up-to-date references of more recent tennis terminology, references to modern players sprinkled in by the editor, reading that prompted Robert to angrily accuse this editor of subverting his work, saying, "You wrote this, I didn't write that!". To counter his response, we agreed to spend an entire filming session with him talking out each chapter. When the transcription was complete, he was presented with exactly what he had said. A this point he became even more angry, shouting, "This is boring!" For years, people have begged for this book to be published, but "careful what you wish for". Ultimately, the book will resemble the unvarnished original more closely with a limited effort to update information or fill in context. In that regard, you are on your own to reconcile the contradictions and occasionally murky language Robert uses to convey thoughts that were chrystal clear in his mind.

Part of the magic of Robert is that he was an anachronism to another age, the old-school Thai, the taskmaster coach who spends more time on molding the character of the player, and creating a coercive atmosphere that forces the subject to become a better problem solver in the moment. The precise expectation was often unclear, except for a strong emphasis on motivation and limited incentives, they would have to make consecutive shots without missing. I have seen the love from a small boy on the court who interpreted Robert's toughness as extreme care for their outcomes. All Robert wanted was the very best of each player. If someone wasn't a great athlete, but they played varsity in high school, he was good with that. It's a myth that Robert qualified players based on talent; in fact, he didn't care about talent much, but hard work was his primary value. Robert's definition of champion is #1 in the world, Grand Slam Title holder, pro level champion. If player's did not quit in the first lesson, usually their outcomes were very good. This editor hopes it helps your outcomes and those of your players to pursue excellence.

Introduction

Over the past few decades, I have coached some of the world's top young players. During that time, I have helped many junior players become champions. But, as you will soon discover, I am not a coach who comes up with fantastic, new ideas that will change the game of tennis. Far from it. I stress the basics. I teach what works, and I get results.

I have included in this book most of the same tips and suggestions that I have given my students over the years. By working hard and following the ideas presented here, you should significantly improve your game. In fact, you will play better tennis than you ever thought possible.

But, do not think that reading this book will automatically make you a champion. Tennis is a highly demanding game that requires many years of dedicated practice to play well. And it is not something that can be done alone. You will need the help and support of your parents. And you will also need professional guidance from a tennis coach. Hard work, cooperation, a willingness to learn, desire, and determination - all these qualities are essential for becoming a champion.

If you are a determined young person who likes excitement and challenge and one-on-one sports contests, then tennis is definitely the game for you. If you are really dedicated, so dedicated that you are willing to sacrifice everything else for it, then you are well on your way to becoming a champion.

Robert Lansdorp 2013

1 - Player Development Director

I was asked in an interview what I would do if I were named the director of player development for the USTA. I would create an atmosphere where they can perform specific drills. I would assess each player's mental toughness and their willingness to work hard, noting significant involvement from parents who, however, did not guide the stroke instruction or interfere with the training. Leave the player with the coach they have, not interrupt that relationship, because that coach is working their ass off. How can we help you? Arthur Ashe never interfered with the players at the beginning of the player development program. USTA should be a supporting system, but it won't happen. Bob Brett was great, having worked with Becker, Ivanisevic, and Cilic, and he ran the program for Juniors in Canada. Bob had me come to Canada to train some juniors, and I still get juniors from Canada that are sent to me to train, but the USTA has never sent me a player. Most likely, it's because they are afraid they won't get the credit for developing the player, and they are worried that the kid will be known as a "Lansdorp Player". It might be because they don't like me, but who cares about that?

Tennis for 10 and under, with the red, orange, and green balls, is not suitable for talented young players; it's more appropriate for 4, 5, and 6-year-olds. It's for not-so-talented players. I want to see the tape of top players playing with transition balls, and how old they were when they did that.

2 - Fast Feet And Patterns Of Play

Move through the ball when you hit, then move to the next ball. Split stepping can cause players to lose the timing of their shot. First, start by getting your racquet ready and making a slight turn. It all comes down to reacting to the ball with your eyes. I had a group of girls; one was faster, and another was slower, but the slower girl still managed to get to the drop shot. We did a lot of speed drills and testing. The faster girl, a track star, didn't pay close enough attention to the ball.

In contrast, the slower girl always seemed to be in the right place, thanks to her faster reactions. Eyes command the feet. The eyes are overlooked like crazy.

Q. Do you teach patterns of play?

No, I teach instinct. Basic patterns, yes, but I don't tell the players how to play; they have to figure that out on their own. We practice and drill, focusing 80% on cross-court shots and 20% on down-the-line shots. When you teach them all the shots, but let them play instinctively, they will find the way to win on the day. Just be sure not to tell them too much.

Q. What do you think of match charting?

Match charting is good, but not too much. I'm interested in first serve percentage, errors, and winners on forehands or backhands - that's it. I don't want too much detail.

Don't degrade a kid; instead, work on the things you need. If you are looking for numerous small things to criticize the kid, you are making a big mistake.

3 - Why You Need A Coach

There is no getting around the fact that if you want to play tennis like a champion, you need the help of a tennis expert of some kind. Most juniors obtain this help by taking lessons from a professional instructor. In fact, I'm not aware of any junior players who become champions without the guidance of a coach or another tennis expert.

Actually, it should go without saying that you need a coach. After all, anyone who wants to become an expert at anything, no matter what it is, usually welcomes help from a person more advanced in the same field. This is what you must do if you want to play tennis like a champion: find a coach with whom you can work and learn everything you can from them. Don't try to do it alone because you can't. Believe me, you'll be amazed at how much your game improves after taking a few lessons from a professional coach.

What To Expect From A Coach

A tennis coach has two main jobs. First, he must be a teacher who can convey his knowledge to the student. Second, he must be a tennis expert, someone who knows the game so well that he can spot mistakes by watching for just a few minutes.

You can do the first job yourself by reading books, watching televised matches, and so on. But the second job is impossible for you to do alone. You need someone else, someone who can stand aside and watch you play, a person who can see the slightest wrong movement, the tiniest mistake, and only a coach can do this. Even more important, a coach can make suggestions to correct your mistakes.

It's best to have a coach from the start when you're just beginning to learn the game. If you go out by yourself and try to develop a game style on your own, you're going to pick up 1 million bad habits. However, if you have a coach teaching you, then they can guide you in the right way to play from the start. Then you won't have to waste a lot of your time and his time breaking all those self-taught bad habits.

I should warn you, however, that there is a side to taking lessons from a coach that you might not like. The most successful coaches are rather strict with their students on the court during lessons. This is not only desirable but necessary. In fact, I'm often criticized for being too strict with my students. My response is always the same: Tennis is a very demanding game, and if my students are unable to handle the pressure of a half-hour tennis lesson, then they certainly will not be able to withstand the stresses of tournament competition.

Most tennis lessons last half an hour, and the number of lessons per week can vary according to your own personal situation. If your parents are actively interested in your game and practice with you daily, or accompany you to lessons, you can likely get by with just one lesson per week. Three lessons a week is the ideal schedule, as it allows sufficient time between lessons to avoid picking up bad habits.

Your coach is a very busy person, so don't expect a lot of personal attention from him off the court. A coach is not your best friend; they are your teacher, and they are running a business. It is his job to teach you to play a better game of tennis, and he will probably not have much time for anything else.

Don't forget, however, that your coach has the same goal as you do. He would like nothing better than for you to become a champion player. Coaches are judged by their students' performance on the court. And you becoming a champion will naturally make your coach look like a winner as well. So, if he asks angrily or is hard to please, it's not because he doesn't like you or wants to see you fail; instead, it's because he wants you to succeed and become a champion. He knows that for you to do that, he must push you harder than you would usually push yourself.

4 - What A Coach Expects From You

A tennis coach expects the same thing from you that most school teachers do. He expects you to be on time, to pay attention to him, and to do your best to follow his instructions. Most tennis coaches also ask their students to do something that few school teachers would dare ask of their pupils: to work hard to improve themselves. If you really want to be a champion, you have to be willing to work constantly to improve your game. Seeing that you do that is part of a coach's job, as it involves teaching you how to hit the ball. Perhaps the most important thing for you to do during a lesson is to make sure you understand everything that your coach is telling you. He is constantly suggesting ways for you to improve your game, and you must understand precisely what he is saying; otherwise, you cannot practice what he has told you. When it comes time for your next lesson, you will still have the same problems to correct. This is a waste of both your time and your coach's time. So, if you don't understand what the coach is telling you, by all means stop him and ask him to explain further.

Ensuring you understand your coach is a crucial step. But I have learned over the years to expect such ingenuity from my students. In fact, after explaining something to them, I often ask if they understand what I said. Almost all of them say yes, but many times they cannot even repeat my words back to me. When that happens, I warn them that they'll face a challenging workout the next time they claim to understand something when they actually don't. After that, most of them decide to start paying closer attention to me. And the next time I stop suddenly and ask them to tell me what I said, they can repeat my words back to me. So then I say, 'Big deal,' and ask them to explain what I said in their own words. Once again, they are often at a loss. They may have been listening to me, but they still didn't understand what I was saying.

* * *

A good example of this is what happened with John Austin. At 15 years old, he was experiencing problems with his backhand. He tended to hit it long and wide. At every lesson, I told him that he was opening up too soon and sliding his racket under the ball, making it go long, and why. Once I would say to him what he was doing wrong, he would quickly correct his mistake. But when the next lesson came, he was back doing the same thing again.

John and I worked on this problem for many weeks. Every time I explained to him precisely what he was doing wrong, he would improve his backhand until the next lesson. John was listening to me, but he was not taking it in. He didn't seem to understand the problem. As a result, he was unable to make any real effort to correct the mistake on his own. He had to rely on me to catch it every time. One day, John came for his lesson, and I told myself, "I'm not going to tell this guy one thing today." At the beginning of the lesson, we greeted each other and proceeded to the court, just as we do in any other lesson. The first thing I did was hit him a couple of balls to his backhand to see if he was still making the same mistake of opening up early and slicing under the ball. As always, the ball went long and wide, but I didn't say a word. Throughout John's entire lesson, I didn't say one word about his backhand. If he hit a forehand, I said "Hey, that's a nice shot!" or something along those lines. However, I did not mention the mistake he repeatedly made with his backhand.

At the end of the lesson, John stomped off the court without saying a word to me. He went to his mother and told her he was fed up with the whole thing, that he had just had the worst lesson of his life, and that he would never take another lesson from Robert Lansdorp again.

Mrs. Austin was usually very warm and understanding as a person. She saw me push her children very hard on the court, but she never protested, because she had always known that I was only making them do what they must do if they wanted to become champions. However, on this particular day, she was pretty upset, yet she still had a good time. She couldn't understand why she should pay me to give John a lesson when I refused to correct his mistakes.

I explained to John and his mother exactly what I was doing. I told them both that John needed to make an effort to understand what I had been explaining to him for weeks. "When you do something wrong.", I said, "You have to realize it yourself without being told, then you have to take the information you've been given and use it to correct the mistake on your own. From now on, I will not remind you repeatedly about an error you are making, unless you are genuinely attempting to correct it on your own.

That was one of the best lessons John Austin ever had. He learned to think for himself on the court, and he knew that to think for himself, he must thoroughly understand what I had told him during the lesson. He realized for the first time that he was on his own, that whatever he did in the game of tennis, he had to do himself. He couldn't rely on me or anyone else. I was just there to help him, to show him the way. The rest was all up to him.

My students know that when they come out to take a lesson with me, they will be pushed to their limit. They know that I will not pity them whatsoever. They know that I won't even care if they get out of breath and can no longer run. They can hyperventilate as far as I am concerned.

It's interesting to see how kids react to this treatment. Some of them start to cry because I'm pushing them so hard. And a few of those who cried even threatened to throw up if I didn't take it easy. I tell them it's hard to scream and throw up at the same time, do one or the other, do it, and get it over with, because I am out here on the court waiting.

The reason I was so cold and heartless is that sooner or later, every junior player must realize that they are entirely alone during the tennis match. Excuses and temper tantrums will not work, and neither will relying on your coach to tell you what to do.

You need to understand what your coaches are telling you, and, more importantly, use that information to correct your mistakes. You must do what your coach tells you to do, not only during lessons but also during practice. And you have to work your tail off, not to please your coach, but to improve your chances for success. Remember that if you don't work hard and follow your coach's advice, you'll be punished. You won't be grounded for the weekend or set to bed without supper or anything like that, but you will suffer just the same. You will not reach your goal of becoming a champion.

5 - The Good Seed And The Project

I have always dreamed of being a plantation owner. I love gardening, planting seeds, and then seeing the result. In some ways, this farming approach has carried over into my coaching, as I focus on the result within a long-range plan. Coaches are also artists. These two roles, as a coach and as an artist, are how I approach each child. Don't get me wrong, while I do mold and shape them (they come to me one way, and they leave another way), I try to instill focus, concentration, consistency, placement, and power on every single shot—the power you can do without, but placing the ball deep is crucial. A good serve and speed, combined with deep shots, can help you make something of yourself. Really, players only cooperate in the ways they want to be molded or shaped into a player or a person. Once a player has had a few lessons with me, they very rarely leave.

Placing the ball deep is crucial.

I challenge the player with a very tough lesson, and if they can get through their initial time with me, then they really want to become a champion. I try to intimidate the kid, but I expect that player to be able to talk with me. Their future working with me hinges on how well they can meet the high level of expectations I have for them. Sure, I yell at kids sometimes, but it's not like I yell every lesson; it's actually very rare that I do. However, I am an expert at creating frustrating situations for them to deal with on court, so they can be well-prepared for anything they might face from an opponent. When we played practice matches, I would even make a few bad calls, because the kids couldn't. Perhaps this is my way of ensuring I never waste my time, theirs, or their parents' money. I prepared them for the fact that they would face bad calls in their junior matches.

My players are well prepared for anything.

My 'art projects,' on the other hand, are subject to many tiny adjustments. When my players are interviewed, they say that they can't remember a single technical piece of advice that I have given them. (It sounds like no one knows how to express the gradual approach to shaping the game.) An example of this is Eliot Teltscher's backhand. He had one of the best backhand timings I have ever seen. He had a remarkable ability to understand the subtle changes I asked him to make and execute them, specifically hitting the ball through and maintaining the follow-through in a certain way. My Way. I'm curious to know which stroke my former players are most proud of in the game. Tracy Austin said that I give the best groundstrokes in the world. The way I teach groundstrokes has evolved, and I am not as dogmatic as people often portray me to be. Just the other day, someone shared a picture mimicking the way I would have taught in the 1970s, which made me laugh along with them. I teach much differently now; the game has changed, so everyone must adapt to it. I train my players to face the challenges they'll encounter in reality, rather than some outdated fantasy world.

I train my players to meet the challenges they will face in reality.

I expect my players to communicate openly with me, without fear, and share their needs and wants. While I may come across as gruff on court, all my players know that I care about them as individuals and as tennis players. What I bring is a vision for the player's potential, but the plan is constantly evolving as we continue. A while back, I was on a Russian Radio Interview, and a 10-year-old boy called in to the show, worried, "I want to play a one-handed backhand, but my coach wants me to hit a two-handed backhand. What should I do?" Without a moment's hesitation, I said, "Fire your coach!". The most important aspect is the player's self-determination and decision-making. When the young player has the wherewithal to speak their own mind, know their own mistakes, and make decisions, that is what makes good seed that will grow strong.

I teach my players to be self-aware about their game.

The players don't all grow up the same. You may notice that some of my players look stylistically similar, but some use one-handed backhands, while others use two-handed backhands. Some players had Eastern grips, while others had semi-western grips. Some played the net quite often, others were pure baseliners. You will notice a fairly wide stylistic variation between Tracy Austin, Pete Sampras, Lindsay Davenport, and Maria Sharapova, as well as some notable similarities.

Contrary to popular belief, I was never a drill sergeant on grips, except for a Western grip. I never wanted to teach anyone who had a Western grip, but later in my career, I had a player who came with a Western grip, and he refused to change. However, it turned out to work fine.

Ultimately, coaching is not about me; it's about the player, and it should probably be that way for every good coach.

6 - The First Meeting: Dealing With Parents

B: When you first meet a player and they're getting out of the car, how does it all begin when you're meeting a player and their parents for the first time?

R: Well, it changes a little bit. If I've never met the person, it depends somewhat on the age of the player and somewhat on my attitude, so it's never the same. It is always a matter of making the kid understand that there's going to be discipline right away. To me, that is an essential part, as I get the discipline right away, which makes my job a lot easier. My reputation, most of the time, precedes me, so I don't really have to stress it as much, as the kids are already paranoid, nervous, whatever, so I don't really have to stress discipline too much, you know, I really don't.

My reputation precedes me.

The way I meet them, just my attitude, it's like Maria said, "it's the look" I give them. I look at them. I ask them a question. I want them to answer the question. I'm very friendly to the parents. When the parents try to answer the kid's question, I won't ask them not to do that. I say, "I want you to be here," because I always want parents to be there. I've never wanted to tell the parents, "I never want you around the court." That happens once or twice because they become so involved and won't shut up. Still, usually I'll tell the parents, "I want you to be here, but I don't want you to coach your kid, or distract them, but I will ask you a question sometimes because I want to make sure you understand what I'm teaching your kid."

I want parents to WATCH the lesson.

Now, if I have a 9- or 10-year-old, or even a 15-year-old, I would like the parents to understand what I'm teaching the child. Especially when the player is younger, I explain it to the parents so they can take the kid out and do precisely the same thing, essentially what I'm doing. So, I want the parents to be there, to understand, and to ask me questions if they're brave enough to do so. They can ask me a question, or I can ask the parent a question, and that's how I do it. I try to keep the parents separate from the kids, for the most part. When I talk to the kid, it's just the kid. When I'm on the court with the kid, I prefer not to have the parents involved. It took him at least 2 years to get used to me being on the court. Yuri started talking to Maria, and I told him to leave.

The first time I meet a player, it's like sizing up a blank canvas. Whether they're a nervous 9-year-old stepping out of the car or a cocky 15-year-old with a racket bag slung over their shoulder, my approach is about setting the tone from the get-go. As a coach, you've got to establish discipline, build trust, and read the player—all in that first hour. Here's how I do it, and how you can too, whether you're a coach or a player starting with a new mentor. Discipline is the cornerstone. When a kid steps onto my court, they need to know I mean business. I don't need to bark orders to prove a point. It's in my look, my tone, the way I carry myself. Maria once said it was "the look" I gave her that set the standard. I'll ask a kid a simple question—maybe about their grip or how they feel about their forehand—and I expect an answer. It's not just about the response; it's about teaching them to think and communicate. Players, when your coach asks you something, speak up. It shows you're engaged. Parents are part of the equation, but they need to understand their role. I'm always polite, welcoming them to stay courtside. I want them to know what I'm teaching, especially for younger players. A 9- or 10-year-old needs reinforcement off the court, and parents can help by echoing my lessons. But I draw a line: no coaching from the sidelines. I'll say, "I want you here, but don't answer for your kid or distract them." If a parent gets too involved, I don't ban them—I just redirect. Once, with Maria Sharapova, it took her dad, Yuri, two years to stop chiming in. Patience is key, but so is clarity. Coaches, set boundaries early. Players, focus on your coach's voice, not your parents'. The first session is about observation.

I watch how the player moves, how the ball comes off their racket, how they carry themselves. Are they timid? Overconfident? Do they listen? I don't overhaul their game on day one. Instead, I introduce fundamentals—clean contact, proper footwork, and a mindset of consistency. For young players, I explain things and involve the parents so they can reinforce at home. For older players, I might challenge them with a drill to test their focus. Coaches, tailor your approach to the player's age and attitude. Players, show up ready to work, not to show off. That first meeting sets the stage for everything. Establish discipline, build a connection, and start with the basics. It's not about flashy shots—it's about creating a player who listens, learns, and fights. That's how champions begin.

7 - Setting The Tone

I create an atmosphere that sends a strong message to my new student. As the new student arrives and gets out of the car, I inform them that I have a lesson right before and will be teaching. I then tell them, "Be ready, because I am going to yell at you." They might ask, "Why?", but I say, "Never mind, I don't mean it, I'm just going to do it."

When the new student arrives, as soon as they get out of the car, I start to yell at my current student, to the effect of, "If you make another stupid mistake, I am going to give you 20 at the baseline, do you want that?" I want to plant in the new player's mind the thought, "I'd better try not to make any mistakes." This is beneficial for them, as it allows them to know from the outset that I have high expectations for the lesson. High expectations from coaches and parents are a crucial component of any pupil's success.

I ask my students questions, and I expect them to be able to answer them. They may struggle to come up with answers, but as long as they are honest in their answer, I don't mind. I want to challenge their thinking because tennis is a lonely game, and you are on your own out there on court. If the player gives me a B.S. answer, I'll really stop and make them think.

What I don't allow is for the parent to answer on behalf of the child. Why would they do that? I don't care what the parent is thinking and how much they know, if it gets in the way of the player learning to speak for themselves. Part of the lessons that prepare a tennis player involves developing independent thought and problem-solving skills. Your parent doesn't hold your hand while you play. In very few matches is there any legal coaching that happens. I'm not fond of the idea of coaching on the WTA tour. Sure, it's fun for people watching TV to see that, but if the player can't figure it out on their own, what's the value of it?

* * *

One of my primary teaching objectives is to give players independence from everyone, allowing them to be their own person on the court. When they take ownership of that, they gain an edge over the players that the other parents and coaches have coddled. Independent decision-makers are more grounded and better equipped to handle adversity than those who are overly dependent on others for anything related to tennis.

When parents have attempted to interject into the lesson, I ask them to leave. Rarely, I have to tell parents to go, and they do, mainly because I don't want them to interfere with the lesson I am coaching. I welcome any comments from them before or after the lesson. One of my favorite items that I still have is a letter from Mrs. Austin, handwritten in 1979 as Tracy Austin was playing in Europe on clay, preparing for the French Open. In it, she mentions having many ideas for Tracy's game. So, of course, I will listen. Who wouldn't listen? Besides, she was there watching, and I was not. The myth that I'm a 'my way or the highway' coach is entirely inaccurate. What is true is that I have high expectations for players to perform to the very best of their ability every moment we are on the court, working on their game.

The tone I set is that I am entirely in control of the lesson atmosphere. Under my control, the player is free to speak their mind, and they had better speak their mind! I do not allow a parent to talk while I am coaching, but I might allow them to ask me a question if it does not disrupt what the player and I are working on. If the parent thinks they are going to run the lesson, then I will send them away. The goal is to create an atmosphere that fosters the best learning environment for the player to thrive.

8 - How Players Must Approach Tennis

Tennis is a lonely game. You play tennis for and by yourself. You congratulate yourself for every win, just as you blame yourself for every loss. Indeed, whether you win or lose a particular match can never mean as much to anyone else in the world as it does to you. This is why your attitude and approach to the game are so important. One way to alleviate the loneliness of tennis is to join a team; however, when you truly embark on the pursuit of serious success in juniors and the lower-level professional circuit, you will discover precisely how lonely it can be.

Time Commitment

How far you go in the sport of tennis depends almost entirely upon your own personal desire and determination. Another significant factor is that an athlete's physical ability plays a substantial role in their success. Ability is something that can be acquired by anyone willing to put in enough time and effort. In other words, it takes desire and determination to develop the necessary skill set to become a champion. So, will you become a champion? No one can answer that question except you.

You need to recognize that you are the one becoming a champion.

The first thing to realize is that becoming a good tennis player requires a specific commitment on your part, a pledge to devote all your free time and energy to the game. You may have already made such a commitment. If not, consider it seriously. Sooner or later, you will have to commit yourself. Otherwise, you will only be the local or club player, you will never be nationally ranked, and you will certainly never be a champion.

Commitment to Learning

Commitment is just one aspect of your overall approach to the game; however, the other significant aspect is the willingness to learn. Many junior players lack the desire to learn. And this is unfortunate, because only by learning can anyone hope to improve their game. There are three people from whom you can expect to learn about tennis. A coach is the most obvious person. Almost all junior players are willing to learn from a coach. Your opponent is another excellent teacher, especially if they are a better player. A future champion is always willing to learn from their opponent. The third and most important of your teachers is yourself. Many juniors are unwilling to learn from their own mistakes, which ultimately leads to failure.

Having a growth mindset is essential to improvement.

You must be willing to examine your own mistakes closely, try to understand them, and work to rectify them. At the same time, you must be able to recognize your strong points, to rely on them, and use them to your advantage. Remember, you are your own best teacher, but only if you are your own best student as well.

I always recognize the juniors with the best attitudes. They are the ones who improve from week to week, and they are eager to learn, practicing diligently. They are willing to hit a thousand balls in half an hour to get a particular shot, to drill it into themselves, to make themselves do it again and again, until they can actually feel it when they are doing it right. They understand the challenges of tennis and are doing their best to master it. They try and try, and that is one of the secrets to their success, what it takes to become a champion. Champions do not appear suddenly and begin to dominate a sport. Without exception, they start at an early age and work diligently to become winners. By the time the general public becomes aware of a successful athlete, they have likely been honing their skills for years, gaining experience, winning some matches and losing others, all while persevering, working diligently, and sacrificing everything for the game. This is what it takes to become a champion.

It will take some sacrifices to become great.

There are two main sacrifices that you must make if you want to play like a champion. First, you must give up most of your free time. Second, you must spend all of your excess energy working to improve your game. Actually, most champions do not view all the time spent and work as a sacrifice; they would rather be working to improve their game than doing anything else anyway, so they are not really sacrificing anything. Either way, there is no escaping the fact that, if you want to play tennis like a champion, you must give up practically all your free time. Tennis is both a mental and physical game, and it takes time to develop both aspects. Cognitive development is a gradual process that occurs with proper training, experience, and intense concentration. Physical development is, by far, the most challenging for everyone, as it requires the most time both on and off the court.

Players must develop their mind and body.

Of course, school already takes up most of your time. This is to be expected. School is, after all, the most critical part of any young person's life, and you must never sacrifice your school work for anything, including tennis. Tennis must be next in importance; however, to play like a champion, you need to dedicate two to three hours to practice every single day. Additionally, you need to establish a daily exercise routine that includes running, jumping rope, and other exercises discussed later in the book. If you add the time that you take practicing and doing exercises, and the inevitable amount of homework that you are doing from school, you can see that there is not a lot of time left in the day. If you are truly dedicated to becoming a champion, you will be willing to do all this and more.

Additionally, you must be willing to push your body to its very limits. You must be able to go that extra distance during that vital match, to play the third set as well as you did the first set. And the only way you can do that is to fully prepare your body beforehand. Pushing yourself this hard is not easy, but every successful athlete does it, and it is a crucial part of preparing to play tennis like a champion.

You will need to find your limits and expand them.

Besides, if you are not fully prepared for an important match, it could be dangerous to you. You could easily hurt yourself if you push yourself too hard. Further than you are physically able to go. This often occurs during tournament play. If, for instance, you're not in top physical shape and you are matched against a better player, or players who can run harder place shots all over the court, then you are in real trouble. Sure, you might be able to keep up with your opponent during the first day's match, but if you have to go against such a player two or three days in a row, then your body will probably start to give out on you. You'll work whole muscles and so on. You won't stand a chance because you are not prepared physically to go all the way.

Quite often, Young players complain to me about losing their concentration during the match. Nine times out of 10, they lost their concentration due to physical exhaustion. They began to think more about their sore legs than their backhand, and as a result, their concentration waned. Pretty soon, their game fell apart, and the match was lost, all because they were unable to push themselves that extra little bit when it counted most.

You can't overestimate how the trained body and mind work together.

I constantly challenge my students, and they are often surprised by what they can achieve. For example, I forced them to come up with good shots when they're physically exhausted, precisely what they must do during a match. First, I put them through a challenging workout. Then, all hit them a short shot over the net. The first time I do this, they usually will not even try for it. They say it's a ridiculous shot, one they could never reach. So I get furious and threaten them, and pretty soon, I think it's better to try for the shot than listen to me rant and rave. If I keep hitting short shots, and they keep trying, they will eventually reach the ball in time. Before too much longer, they can put the ball away, the very same shot they said was ridiculous.

You need to be prepared to go further than you think possible. When you're tired, when you're completely worn out, when you're ready to give up and go home, that's when you have to come up with a good shot, the winning shot, the put-away shot. Coming up with the right shot at the right time is one of the most valuable and necessary talents for a champion. But it is not a talent that magically appears out of nowhere. It is acquired slowly through perseverance and determination. Through many long years of hard work and an overpowering urge to be number one.

9 - Shaping A Champion: Tracy Austin

When I first laid eyes on Tracy Austin, she was a pint-sized 7-year-old with a fierce glint in her eye, gripping her racket with two hands on both sides. I'd just arrived at the Kramer Club in Los Angeles, fresh off coaching in San Diego, where I'd turned raw kids into players who dominated Southern California. I didn't have a coaching degree or a stack of manuals—I coached by instinct, guided by what I'd learned from my own playing days and a knack for spotting potential. Tracy was my first big test at Kramer, and she became a cornerstone of my legacy, proof that my gut-driven approach could forge a Grand Slam champion.

The San Diego Roots: Building Confidence

Before Tracy, I cut my teeth in San Diego, coaching kids like Walter Redondo, a 12-year-old phenom so good that players in L.A. would track him down just to see him hit. Walter was a natural, and working with him gave me confidence. I didn't overthink it—I just did what felt right: emphasize discipline, clean technique, and mental toughness. I never read coaching books or studied theories. I'd watch a kid hit, listen to the ball off their strings, and adjust based on what I saw and heard. By the time I got to Kramer, my San Diego kids were beating L.A.'s best, and I knew I was onto something.

At Kramer, I wasn't impressed by the talent pool. Most kids were just kids—nothing special. But Tracy? She stood out from the first ball she hit. At 7 or 8, she was intense, coachable, and fiercely competitive. If I praised another player, she'd crank her shots harder, like she was saying, "I'm better." That fire made her a coach's dream. Players, take note: that kind of drive—wanting to prove yourself every day—is what sets you apart. Coaches, look for that spark in your players. It's the raw material of greatness.

***

The Two-Handed Dilemma: Trusting Instincts

The 1970s were a different era in tennis. The two-handed backhand was rare—Chris Evert was one of the few making it work. Tracy came to me with a two-handed grip on both sides. Her forehand was awkward, so I switched it to a one-hander right away. It wasn't easy for a 7-year-old, but Tracy adapted fast, learning to drive the ball with control and power. Coaches, don't be afraid to make bold changes early if a shot doesn't fit. Players, trust your coach when they push you to adjust—it's about building a game that lasts.

Her two-handed backhand was another story. I briefly considered changing it to a one-hander to match the era's trend. Everyone else had one-handers—Walter's was a thing of beauty. But Tracy's backhand was special. Her returns of serve, even as a little girl, were precise and fearless. I remember watching her rip a return and thinking, "This is perfect." Thank God I trusted my gut and left it alone. That backhand became her best shot, a weapon that carried her to two US Open titles. Coaches, know when to leave a strength alone. Players, lean into what comes naturally—it's your edge.

Building Toughness: The Tracy Way

Tracy's mental toughness was unreal. I've coached champions like Pete Sampras and Maria Sharapova, but Tracy, at 8 years old, was in a league of her own. She'd fight through any drill, no matter how grueling. One day, I pushed her hard in a session, and she hyperventilated, gasping for air. Her mother sat courtside, calm as ever, while I told her, "Next time, bring a paper bag—she'll breathe through it." I wasn't being mean; I was teaching Tracy that she could push past her limits. She never complained, never backed down. That's what made her special.

***

People misunderstand my approach. They think I'm some drill sergeant, barking orders and breaking kids down. That's nonsense. My goal isn't to punish—it's to build. With Tracy, it was a process. I'd set up drills, make them tougher, and she'd fight harder. If I raised the bar, she'd claw her way over it. I didn't plan to "toughen her up"—it happened naturally because she was wired to compete. Coaches, create challenges that push your players' limits without crushing their spirit. Players, embrace the grind. Every tough session is a chance to grow stronger.

Instinct Over Theory: Keeping It Simple

What set Tracy apart was her trust in my system. I didn't overcomplicate things. My technique came from my own playing days—I knew what a clean hit felt like, how a ball should sound off the strings. I'd watch Tracy, adjust her footwork, or tweak her swing path, all based on instinct. It worked because she did everything I asked, no questions. If I said, "Hit it harder," she'd crank it. If I said, "Stay low," she'd drop her center of gravity. Her simplicity made my job easy.

I read coaching articles on social media now, and I laugh. People overanalyze, throwing around buzzwords and theories. With Tracy, and later Pete, it was straightforward: discipline, clean technique, and relentless effort. My system wasn't rocket science—it was about getting the basics right and letting the player's talent shine. Coaches, don't get lost in technical jargon. Focus on what works: solid fundamentals and a player who listens. Players, don't overthink your game. Master the basics, and the rest will follow.

The Blueprint for Champions

Tracy's journey wasn't just about talent—it was about building a mindset. She came to me loving tennis, thanks to Vic

Braden's fun approach, but I gave her the tools to dominate. By 16, she was a US Open champion, the youngest ever at the time. Her two-handed backhand, relentless returns, and mental toughness carried her there. But it started with that 7-year-old girl who fought for every point, who listened to every word I said, and who never let a challenge break her.

For coaches, Tracy's story is a lesson in trusting your instincts. You don't need a PhD in biomechanics to develop a champion. Watch your player, listen to the ball, and adjust based on what you see. Build discipline early, but don't crush their spirit—guide them to find their own toughness. For players, Tracy's path shows what's possible when you commit fully. Show up ready to work, embrace challenges, and trust your coach's plan. Talent gets you started, but discipline and fight make you a champion.

Tracy Austin was one of the toughest kids I ever coached, and her success proved my approach worked. No books, no overthinking—just instinct, hard work, and a kid who refused to quit. That's the blueprint for building a champion, and it's as true today as it was in 1975.

10 - Testing For Understanding

B: How do you test for learning and understanding?

R: I think first of all, that's why it takes a long time, it takes a long time to get a feel for what the kid is all about. I don't want to say necessarily that a kid who doesn't listen is not the brightest; I don't have *that* much experience. I usually find that the very bright kid is also the kid who listens well. In other words, if they listen well, they're very coachable. I've always said that great champions, or great players, are very coachable, and it's not like pulling teeth. Therefore, we come back to the point: what they do is they listen right away, they understand what you're saying, they analyze it in their head, and they *do* it, and you don't have to repeat it over and over and over again. The kids who are more challenging to work with are those who don't quite listen, don't reasonably analyze it, and it takes a longer time to develop; it requires more effort on my part. Recognizing that they're not listening to you, you bring it up more often to quiz them on the material being taught. You say, "Okay, what did I say?"

I do a lot of questioning.

It's the whole combination of what they do when they're not on the tennis court. What do they do at school? It's almost the same in a way, and I cannot necessarily change that. See, I can make the parents aware of the fact that when I say to them, "Your child is not quite listening, focusing on the words I'm saying, they don't absorb, they just listen to the sounds, and they don't want ever to accept what I'm saying," Therefore, as a coach you have to repeat yourself more. You have to correct them more often, and it makes it more difficult. It's just a matter of recognizing this, and again, that's where the discipline comes in. If the kid is a little afraid of the consequences of not listening to you—that doesn't mean you have to beat them up—but, you know, if you give them '20 at the baseline' and they don't like it, it's good for them anyway. They feel like, "I'd better listen to the guy because I don't want to get my 20 at the baseline," then you can get somewhere with them. That's why I think discipline is essential. You can say, "What am I saying?" and the kid might say something stupid that you never even said. "Okay, you're not even listening to what I'm saying, now give me 20." The player gets '20' enough times, and they start saying, You know, I'd better start listening to the guy". And it's just the whole combination of focusing, listening to what the coach says, understanding what he says, what I say, putting it to work for you, and it makes it a lot easier.

B: So you aren't babysitting?

It doesn't make any difference whether the kid is 4 years old or 14 years old. When they come to me, they have to perform—it's as simple as that. They have to listen and take action. I'm skilled at analyzing kids, quickly understanding what they're all about. It doesn't matter if they are a beginner; I don't pat them on the back. Some coaches might say, "Oh, you're a beginner," and then treat them differently — no 'do what I tell you, listen...'. My court is intense basically all the time, but the good kids don't mind it; they like it. They actually like it, you know, the lazy kid doesn't want to do it, yeah, that kid might not like it, but the good kid, the kid that wants to get better, they like it, they like the attention. All this talk about go hit tennis balls and have fun —that's the biggest B.S., but I don't mind having fun, but if that's the kind of thing you're gonna spend 80% of your time doing on a tennis court, that won't help develop a great player, so if you wanna have fun, that's fine with me. I'm the person who is always intense, and always trying to get from point A to point B, always trying to improve the player better and better to try to develop them, and I know what it takes to create. It doesn't take constant praise of a player with "Oh, that's so great, that's so great" all the time; instead, I take the kid apart mentally and physically.

11 - Uniquely Gifted Athletes

B: I spoke with Eliot Telstcher for 30 minutes, and he said the same things as Tracy Austin about the way you shaped his groundstrokes, that you gave him a lot of toughness, but it wasn't like you were yelling at him all the time. He said it was fun, or he would not have stayed. So tell us a little about Elliot.

R: Basically, that's who I am: I'm so off the wall that sometimes something is happening and it's funny or ... and so it's not like every day they come out and I'm yelling. The way I was, the way I walked on the court, the way they walked on the court with me, it was my presence. Did that instill toughness in the kids right away? Because all of my kids were tough. They were and they are. Some were great, some were not, but they were all tough, whether discussing champions or top 10 players. Sometimes I wonder, "Is that because of the way I was, or is it because I seemed gruff, or I seemed to show a lot of confidence? What was it that they all worked for me and became mentally tough?" I don't really know what it was, because I was mentally tough.

Work Ethic and Long-Term Success

Elliot was one of those kids, again, who had a world-class work ethic. I always liked Elliot, even when he was a pro, because he got to where he was through pure desire. He wasn't a great athlete, but he achieved his goals with determination. I remember working with him, and he was a skinny runt. I mean, when he was 13 or 14, he had no muscle at all, basically skin and bones. He was always competing against bigger boys. People would say, "Oh, so-and-so is going to be much better than Elliot because he's so much bigger and stronger."

I'd say, "Look at Elliot—he times the ball so well, he hits the ball so cleanly. You gotta have some patience until he gets a little stronger." When he was 14, he had a decent one-handed backhand, and as it developed, it became one of the most excellent one-handed backhands of his era. I still think it was better than Federer's. When he was 14, his backhand wasn't phenomenal yet. The way he hit the ball was perfect, so everything in his backhand was just a matter of giving it time—let it develop, let him get stronger. Elliot was a hard worker; all his matches were fight, fight, fight. Who he was fighting for, I have no idea.

A fighting spirit is a great asset.

In contrast, Tracy Austin was fighting for me a lot—she wanted to please me. I don't know what he—he was unbelievable, what a fighter he was. I always use him as an example of how you can become great just by fighting because he didn't have the athletic ability, didn't have a huge serve, and that's why he often lost to Connors and never won a Grand Slam, but he still had an incredible career. He was in the top ten for about 8 or 9 years; it seemed like he never dropped out. The one thing I always remember about Elliot is that when he was 10 years old, I was married then and had step-children. Elliot would always ask me how my family was. It was strange—having a young kid ask about my family—but he always had that in him. Sometimes I think I was lucky; I knew what I was doing. But for him to execute that one-handed backhand—I wish I could have bottled his backhand and sold it. His father always told me, "Robert, why don't you just make that your pet project—hitting a one-handed backhand? Because his one-handed backhand was so good." Whatever I did, it always worked. I never had to think about it—I just did it, and it worked.

12 - Timing The Ball

B: What do you look for to see what the upper limit is for a player's talent?

R: One of the main things that many coaches overlook is the matter of timing the ball. Every great player times the ball exceptionally well. And a lot of the coaches, if not 90%, don't understand the timing. There was a video on Facebook, I don't know, maybe I wasn't too nice in the way I commented on it, a video in which they showed Maria (Sharapova)'s forehand. They showed the so-called 'perfect forehand' that Maria hit. But it wasn't a perfect forehand. The video wasn't that bad, I mean, it wasn't a horrible, like "what is wrong with you?" kind of video, you know, it was actually pretty good. What they neglected to mention is how late Maria hit the ball, and probably the only place she could have gone with the ball is to hit down the line, which was 90% of Maria's problem. She could only go down the line with a forehand. When you try to show Maria's forehand, it's great when you show her hip rotation, but when you don't mention how late she's hitting the ball, and the only choice she has is hitting the ball down the line, then people get the wrong idea. Her timing has limited her. Maria was one of the people—and she deserves a lot of credit—she's the one person who became great without having great timing on the forehand side. Her backhand side timing was unbelievable, and her forehand side timing was lousy from day one. Pete Sampras' timing was impeccable, regardless of the situation. Lindsey Davenport's timing was incredible. She could hit the ball so unbelievably well —controlled, hard— and that all comes with timing.

Part of that is the eyes. 90% of the coaches don't understand that, because I don't even know entirely from experience whether the right eye is stronger than the left when tracking. They track the ball a little late, and they can hit the forehand late. I don't know what came first, Maria doing this, or coaches teaching it... Many coaches now focus on hitting the forehand down the line, and they have the kid hit the ball down the line too often. Every ball goes forehand down the line, and what happens is it becomes a very, very good shot. It's first of all a flatter ball, which is interesting because they're not going to hit the ball five feet over the net. The lines are not five feet over the net; they're low over the net. So the ball goes flatter, and they actually hit the ball a little late, and they hit great down the line, but they can't hit the ball crosscourt very well, and Maria had that problem. With Maria, I had her hit a reverse forehand. You see, like with Pete, I didn't have to, but Pete did; Pete hit reverse-forehands on his own. I have an interesting story about Pete, which I'll share later, regarding his reverse forehand.

B: What do you think of the concept of the contact point being approximately 45 degrees away from you?

R: I don't go with degrees; it's too difficult for me to figure that out.

B: Because it takes measuring?

R: It takes measuring, and you gotta talk to a kid about 45 degrees. I don't even know what 45 degrees means, so could you please explain? It's too—it's not natural anymore. It's not natural, you have to start thinking about 45 degrees here—it's not natural, and I don't go with all that kind of stuff.

B: But out in front, you talk about—

R: Well, you would like to hit the ball out in front, you know, if it's a solid shot out in front. Again, if you used the continental grip, you could hit the ball late. See, people don't know that. People don't know that because it's outdated, you know, you gotta be 77 years old to be able to understand that you usually hit with the continental grip, which means you hit the ball late. And with the grip changed to the Western grip, you have to hit the ball very early. Maria hits the forehand like she should have a continental grip. That's how she believes she hits it, okay? But she doesn't. Now you have to open up and hit the ball early. Or, for Maria's case, she could hit a reverse-forehand. That's what a lot of people do, whether they have to or not. Maria had to; Maria had no option.

B: Earlier, you mentioned that you would give her cross-court targets that would force her to come forward a little bit more.

R: (with a wry smile) I never said that. You said that, I never said that. I said I might have her hit cross-court shots, so she could feel like she had to hit the ball earlier, and when to aim the ball. So she could feel her racquet face aiming a little bit more to where the target is, so she's not hitting, dragging her racquet face, but her racquet face is actually coming through. That's why I do it: so she has to aim the ball. The timing has to be very good; the better your timing, the more consistent and accurate you become. Those are crucial parts, and all those people timed the ball exceptionally well. Some people time the ball extremely well, but perhaps they were lacking in certain areas and only became #10 or #20 in the world, never reaching #1.

13 - Consistency, Placement and Power

I want the kids to take their shots from a nice, deep position in the court repeatedly. The misconception about me is that all my players have to be powerful. Of course, I strive to develop influential players, but I tell them that if they have to sacrifice something between consistency, placement, and power, they don't need the power. What I really want is for my pupil to have the ability to take any ball they receive and hit it repeatedly with depth, and mainly crosscourt. I don't want my players to miss. If they miss more shots than they should, then we can discuss that. I ask them if they have ever heard of Pythagoras, but I try not to say his name right, so they don't start thinking too much about math class. What I want them to figure out on their own is the length of the court along the diagonal length from one corner to the other, along the hypotenuse of a triangle. The court is a rectangle, but the game is played in triangles. Playing crosscourt is so fundamental to reducing errors; it would be stupid not to hit most groundstrokes that direction. Ultimately, tennis is about not missing your shot.

Use the full length of the court diagonally.

When players start to miss too many shots, I begin asking them questions, and then I have them play a game with me. First, I ask them, "If you lose a point to me, how many points do you have to win to get ahead?" Yes, that's right, the answer is two points. What if you didn't lose a careless point in the first place? Then you would only need one point to get ahead. To dramatize this for them, I get some money out of my pocket, and it might be $100 in $20s, and I say, "OK, I'm going to give you one, then you give me two." We do that repeatedly, then I laugh and say, "Look, man, you're broke, out of money, and you lost the match." They seem to really get it after that.

I have had some successful players who had little or no power on their groundstrokes, but because they rarely miss and keep the ball deep crosscourt for the most part, they win a lot of matches. However, if you lack power, then you have to make up for it in other ways. Without a power game, you'd better have a really good serve, a good return of serve, and be pretty fast, because you are going to have to run down the faster ball of your opponent. If the player has a good serve and is fast around the court, then they can make something of themselves. A good example of this is Kei Nishikori, who hits the ball fairly hard but has excellent consistency and speed, with good placement.

One of the main ways I teach this consistency is by using targets. While I do use targets that are on the court, so the player can see where the ball lands compared to the target, it's more important to use a target that is at the net. I have a stick that I put through the net, and it's about 5' tall. I like to put a ball, a can, or some other object that will go on the top as something to hit. It's a tiny target, so it's hard to hit. When players find themselves hitting short, they ask me if they should hit higher, and I say no. Then, I tell them to hit it harder in the court. Maria Sharapova once hit the ball 8 times in a row. When I place targets on the ground for a groundstroke, I never remember them closer than 3' from the baseline or singles sideline, because there should always be some margin of safety. With fewer players, I will make the target a little easier. I expect every player to know where their shots go in relation to the target. It's the only way to learn how to hit it where you want it, and it takes many, many balls.

Try a broomstick with a ball can, stuck through the middle of the net.

I am hearing about a new theory that most pro points last four shots, but if that is all the information they get, then you are going to screw up a lot of coaches and players, because you are telling them to end the point in the first four shots. So, if you provide that information, you'd better really explain it, and coaches should explain it to kids that you have to be able to hit 20-25 balls in a row the same way. Otherwise, you make kids think they only need to hit four shots. It's the wrong information without explanation, and how to develop it. When you share that information without explanation.

The model that people should look at is Djokovic, because he has taken the game to a new level by executing his serves, returns, and positioning perfectly for almost every shot. His movement is also amazing. He is not the most powerful player on the tour.

14 - CPP: A Conversation

B: Tell us about your CPP acronym and how that is the core of your philosophy for coaching.

R: It sounds like a freaking lung disease. "What do you have?" "Well, I got CPP." "Okay."

B: COPD.

R. I know. So I have CPP, and I hope I get over it. Anyway, it's Consistency, Placement, Power; those are the three things I think you have to have. As you can see, my first point is consistency. When people say about me, "Well, he just wants you to hit the ball hard," that's not the case. I want you to hit the ball hard, and I want consistency. Hitting hard and missing 20% of the shots does not work. Forget it. Go higher if you hit it in the net; hit it higher over the net. If you hit it long, put some spin on it, get it into the court, and maintain consistency. Suppose the only way you can hit a consistent ball is by hitting it five feet over the net with topspin. In that case, you have to do something else, or become extremely fast playing on the clay—don't play on the grass, go play on the clay—become extremely fast, and you might be able to do something. If you hit too high and too slowly, then you will have to play better defensively. If you're very consistent and your placement is good, you can actually go quite high in the sport. Especially with the women, if you move well, you're consistent, keep the ball deep, and don't use too much power; look at Wozniacki. She was freaking #1 in the world, and that's a great example of a girl who has a good backhand, a mediocre forehand, no pace, is very quick, fights like hell, and she was #1 in the world, but never won a Grand Slam.

Making the shot is always the most important priority.

So I start with "consistency". I don't care, don't tell me that Robert Lansdorp wants you only to hit the ball hard regardless of where the ball goes; that's about as dumb as you can get. It ultimately comes down to consistency, and then placement follows. Well, the basic placement is to keep the ball deep. We're not talking about angles yet; that's a little bit more advanced. We're talking about getting the ball deep and placing it well consistently. Then, the third one is power. I always tell the kids, "If you have to do away with one of the three, do away with the power." I mean, if you can be very consistent and keep the ball deep, you can actually go a long way and do quite well. You have to have the power to become great. To achieve greatness, you need to have the power.

Therefore, what is important to me is to start developing power at a young age while also developing consistency. That's why I like to work with targets, so a player can get a feel for where to hit the ball to keep it over the net. To me, it's crucial that when the kid hits the ball, they know where the ball is going. They can hit the ball 2 feet over the net, or 3 feet over the net, and they can do that 30-40 times, no problem, and they're excellent. If they don't have the feel, then they start making errors, and you have to get the ball a little higher over the net to achieve consistency. To become great, you must have consistency, always consistency. Second, its placement (you become better, and you get it in three-quarters). The third is power.

B: How do you define the depth? I mean, is there a certain point in the court where you say, "That ball is deep," and then "That ball is too short in the court"?

R: What do you mean? That's a dumb question. (Matter of

factly) You know what deep is. Well, for somebody who doesn't understand it, okay.

R: Well, anywhere between 3-4 feet from the baseline, I would consider that deep. That is, if it has a little bit of pace on it; if it's just a sitter, it has to be a little deeper.

B: So you're saying the last 4 feet of the court?

R: Yeah, somewhere in that area. Shorter than that is no good, but deeper than that, unless you can consistently make it deep, some people try to hit the ball deep and end up hitting it long all the time. So deep that they get balls called out all the time. The depth is significant, and then the power, and that's where I have a lot of people disagreeing with me, or they know it better, they think.

If you start a kid young with the power, you will have no problem. If you start them late, you're gonna have a problem. What you have to do is start them young, so that by the time they're 12, 13, they have so much confidence that they can hit the ball hard, deep, and whatever they want. If you wait, you're gonna lose it; they're gonna lose the confidence to do it. That is a crucial thing that many parents dislike; they don't want their child spending time, because sending them to an academy is seen as a lost cause. Sending your kid to an academy, they'll never learn. Maybe Bollettieri is different because you have the forehand weapon or stuff like this now, or something like that.

B: You mean Bolletieri's The Killer forehand?

R: Killer forehand. But at least they hit the ball. At least he taught these kids to hit the crap out of the ball. With most academies, you get a kid after three years, and they're all more consistent, but they can't put a ball away. It rarely happens when you get a kid out of an academy, he's ripping balls left and right, and what is different is Russia. You get Russian kids, 12 years old, and they all hit the ball hard. They don't even know what an academy ball is or anything; they don't know how to spell it. It doesn't exist! Over here, everybody has an academy, and everybody hits academy balls. That's the downfall of tennis in the United States: the rise of academies.

15 - Pistols And Rifles: Hitting Through The Ball

B: Why is hitting through the ball so important?

R: What I do is I compare—I ask the kids, "Do you know the difference between a pistol and a rifle?" It may take a while for them to be able to explain the difference. So, finally, they give me a difference, and I ask, "What is the difference?" and they may say, "A pistol is short and a rifle has a long barrel." I say, "Do you see that pole over there? Three hundred feet away, see that little light? You could stand there with a pistol, and you cannot even aim and hit something 50 feet away from you. With a rifle, with a long barrel, a sharpshooter can hit that. The longer barrel gives you more power, which in turn gives you more accuracy.

When you hit the ball, drive through the ball like it's a rifle." You know, they used to say, "Line up four balls." You would line up four balls. "Hit through all four balls." In the old days, it was simple because, by following through up front with your eastern or continental grip, you could perfect hitting through the ball. Then, the grips changed, but you can still follow through around your neck; however, the follow-through started to change slightly. In fact, Federer was one of the first players I actually saw who changed his follow-through and it finished downward. I attended two Davis Cup matches between the United States and Switzerland in Basel, and I noticed, I said, "God, you guys, it's too easy." You know, but he was following through more around his midsection, not around his neck. The power generated in the racquets and everything else becomes so great that when they start following through, the ball floats on them. As a result, great players began to follow through a little bit more, and then with the topspin. It was actually easier to follow through by going down a little bit more, rather than up. The more extreme the grips become, the more difficult it is to bring the arm up around the neck; it doesn't work correctly. Players with more extreme grips have to follow through more. Some people follow through almost to the hip; that's how far down they go. Nowadays, it's a trick of still being able to hit through the ball, so with an eastern grip like Federer, he can actually hit through the ball better than somebody with an extreme grip. And so his follow-through is more at the waist; when he drives, he doesn't hit it with extreme topspin. Instead, he hits a little topspin on his drive, and it's a solid drive. When starting with a player, what I looked for was, first of all, to look at the grip. If the kid is 11 years old, I'm not going to fool with the grip; it's not a possibility to change it, it's impossible. Don't waste time and have your kid change. I had a kid, I had a boy, he was 12 or so, he was #1 in the nation, and he had these extreme grips on both sides, and he said, "Robert, I want to change my grips," and I was inexperienced 30 years ago, and I said, "Sure." I mistakenly thought I could do it all, you know? And I worked with the kid for six months, helping him develop an eastern grip, and man, he's hitting the ball well. (Good job, Robert!) He goes and plays his first tournament, and he's right back into extreme grips because he had no confidence in the new grips. I try not to teach players the extreme grip, but you do get kids who come with an extreme grip. Learning to hit the ball with an extreme grip is far more difficult. The only way you can do it is by following through a little bit; you can't follow through too much. Extreme grip players put topspin on it and then follow through down, and then you get a pretty good hit through the ball.

The problem with that grip always will be that when you get a fast low ball, you're up a creek, and I think that's what happened with Nadal. Toni didn't know anything about tennis; he knew how to kick a soccer ball, but don't tell me Toni knew what he was doing when it came to developing a tennis player. Mentally, physically, all that: yeah, Toni knew what he would have Nadal do, but stroke-wise, I don't think he knew exactly what was happening. I believe Nadal came on the court as a little kid, had his racquet down because of the extreme grip, and started hitting the ball with the extreme grip. They realized that, if you reverse the forehand with an extreme grip, it's a heck of a lot easier than when you hit with a regular stroke. So that's why Nadal, I think, started hitting the reverse-forehand much of the time. And his backhand, his grip was standard, so he could hit the ball flat; he actually hits the ball differently on the forehand and the backhand - the backhands are flat. I think you have to look at the person and try to have them hit the ball through them. That doesn't mean that I get a kid with an extreme grip; that I don't put a target two and a half feet above the net, I do, and have the kid drive 100 balls low to the net. Once you work on it, you can actually hit a pretty hard ball; not pure flat, but relatively flat and hard. You can get it with the feel, but it's a lot easier with an eastern grip. The backhand always seems the more straightforward to drive through the ball; the grips are not as extreme, not ...screw around and try to get these grips over because of the topspin, and I think it's screwing a lot of kids up. You've got to drive through the ball more.

Editor's Note: If you also throw in the difference between a musket and a rifle, it has a bearing on understanding balls in flight. A musket pellet did not spin and thus knuckled through the air. In contrast, a rifle spins the bullet, and thus is more accurate, so Robert's allusion to using just enough topspin to keep the ball in the court is a great one, because it also creates more accuracy in the flight of the ball due to Bernoulli's Principle

16 - Player Idiosyncrasies, Birth Of New Technique: The Reverse Forehand

R: One day, I was with Sampras, feeding him fastballs. He's at the baseline, and I'm around the service line, there, feeding balls fast. One ball skids on the line, and he hits it reversed. (I have a video somewhere; I wish I were more organized and had it, and) He's hitting it and I'm yelling at him, "What the hell's the matter with you? What are you doing?" I said, "Why don't you move and drive the ball normally?" He argued, "Robert, the ball was skidding on the line." I answered back to him, "I don't give a damn, just move your feet and drive it." I have another tape, maybe six months later, and I'm running him corner to corner, he's hitting every forehand reversed. I'm never saying a word because I actually learned how the reverse was really working, as he hit a lot of reverse forehands. A lot of coaches could never figure out, "What is he doing? The ball is curving into the court." You know, they never could figure it out, they still didn't want to talk about the reverse forehand. It's a bad word to use; they didn't use it for a long time. The guy hits the most incredible passing shot, reversed, and they don't talk about it. Approach shots are the same way. Let's put a strong emphasis on that because I think it helps people; it saves kids, maybe, ten points a match. Maria would never have won Wimbledon without her reverse forehand, not a chance. The funny part was that Serena did not hit a reverse forehand early on; then later in her career, she did. For Serena, the ball was coming so fast that her timing was so bad, and she missed a lot of forehands. Let's emphasize the reverse forehand, showing exactly what happens, specifically the short follow-through versus the long. Like Sampras, Nadal always has a short follow-through; however, it varies depending on where the ball is. If the ball is short, he has a short follow-through; Maria has a long follow-through, but even when the ball is short, she shortens it up, but it's a shot that everybody has to have. If somebody hits the ball a little late, then there's no better way of hitting the ball than hitting it more reverse. If you have spent a lot of time trying to hit the ball early and it's not happening, it's not gonna happen, so I think we should put some emphasis on teaching the reverse.

B: Is there a specific part of the technique of hitting a reverse forehand that's important to keep in mind?

R: Not really, it's actually a straightforward shot. That's another thing about it, you don't even have to think about it. You may need to explain how you achieve more spin or how you generate more pace.

You see, Capriati had a great reverse forehand. If you actually looked at a tape of her hitting forehands reversed, she hit the ball flat as could be, reversed, so if you come through the ball more before you come up, it becomes a flatter reverse. If you come up right away, it becomes more of a topspin reverse forehand. If you want to hit a lob, that's the best way to hit a lob. That's how you can change it, you don't have to have a reverse forehand that sits high, you gotta actually have a put-away reverse, and a lot of the players do it.

17 - Simplicity, Swing Paths, Social Media

B: Now, there are some notions out there about addressing the ball differently based on being in different parts of the court and other kinds of balls coming into a player's position on the court. How does the shape of the shot change based on where you are on the court?

R:(a little agitated) God, you make it so complicated, you know? It's not all that complicated. First of all, as a viewer, you need to be cautious of people posting all this content on Facebook. Like they had a Facebook thing about Maria's forehand and I mean the video wasn't bad, I mean shouldn't probably be ragging on the video at all, the guy was some Australian—sounded like an Australian, could have been South African, I don't know what the hell the guy was—but the video wasn't bad, but what they lacked to mention was that Maria was hitting the ball late and probably hit every ball relatively flat down the line; they didn't say it. They talked about the rotation of the hips, alright, okay, great, rotation of whatever, and all that other stuff is great, [but] they forget entirely about saying, "I want you to notice now that she was hitting the ball extremely late. She was hitting the ball behind her almost, and she's hitting the ball flat, and it's going down the line." They didn't ever mention that, so when people look at that video, they think that's how you hit a forehand, but maybe that's how you hit a forehand when you hit the ball late and you go down the line.

The basics of technique do not change.

Then there's a guy who has seven different forehands. If you want to show seven different forehands, I have no problem with it. Explain why they're hitting this forehand and that forehand. Having seven different kinds of forehands is wild, to say the least. I could see you having a high forehand, where you bring your arm up, versus a low ball, where you bring your arm down a little bit more. The basic motion remains the same; it doesn't significantly alter your follow-through or stroke. If a ball doesn't bounce up, you have to adjust slightly, but you don't change the stroke; the stroke has to stay the same. Federer didn't change his strokes; his follow-through was basically the same, and his stroke was essentially the same.

Performing instinctively is the goal, not deciding between seven forehands.

Now explain to the people what you're doing, what you're trying to accomplish, and that if your follow-through is down, your follow-through should be in that area on any ball. So basically, you'll have one follow-through here and one follow-through there. You go nuts if you keep changing it; it has to be the same. When you play, it has to become automatic; you play by instinct. When you start thinking about your stroke, you're screwed; nothing is gonna happen. When you have to think about, "Oh, this ball I better follow-through here, or this ball I better follow"—you're a lost cause, completely lost, okay? So you can explain the stroke, which I have no problem with, but don't let people believe that you have to have all these strokes for one person. This person hits it this way, that person hits it another way. What I have a kid do is this: they have to hit me a regular drive, a regular forehand drive, they have to hit me a reverse, and the next ball they have to hit me a regular slice, and then the fourth ball is a crazy slice; they have to change the grip and add a lot of spin on it, the next ball is a regular drive again, so they have to learn to change the grips, but the stroke of the drive is the stroke of the drive, it's the same motion. I do understand when the ball comes high, you may bring it up a little bit more, but you're not going to have one ball where the ball goes high and you bring your racquet up, and one ball where you bring your racquet down. Look at that one guy, Gulbis, look at how he brings his racquet back. Do you think that Gulbis guy was actually worried about where the ball is high or low? No, he hits the same way; he hits the same ball. So on these videos, what you've gotta watch out for when you put these videos on is that you explain what the purpose is, what you're trying to accomplish, because one person with a different kind of strokes is a lost cause, let me tell you, they start thinking about the strokes, it's over.

18 - Confidence And Intimidation?

B: How do you develop confidence in a player?

R: You know, I don't really know for sure. I believe that some people are born with confidence, others understand what confidence is all about, and some are always insecure. That Facebook stuff is just driving me crazy. The other day, I saw something where a coach was asking, "How do I intimidate my opponent?" And I didn't even want to get involved, and I didn't. That's not how it works. See, you don't try to intimidate your opponent. You walk around, and your presence exudes confidence. Your walk, your posture, everything is showing that you have confidence. Then, when you go and start hitting, you actually start hitting the ball with confidence, and you don't make errors right away; you make no errors. And all of a sudden, the person says, "Oh my, this guy is really tough, he's not making any errors". Then you actually get a reputation. Now you have acquired a reputation for being mentally tough, and you walk onto the court. I used to have a girl named Stephanie Rehe; she was unbelievable. She walked through the court with confidence, demanding like she was the boss, but without a nasty attitude. She decided where she was going to sit, and she was running the show, and she was great. And so you don't have to be nasty to your opponent, but you're just showing a significant amount of confidence.

Confidence is all about your attitude;
people might be intimidated by it.

So how do you build confidence? You build confidence by mastering the shots. If you can hit forehands and backhands accurately and consistently, without missing, then you will have confidence. However, if you then play and receive a faster ball, and you're not yet accustomed to it, and you miss the ball, you will lose confidence. As a coach, I take them out and start feeding them faster balls until they get used to them and develop an unbelievable confidence that they won't miss. The confidence comes from being able to control your own game, and then you can control your opponent's game. But you cannot try to intimidate your person—it doesn't work like that. You threaten them with your presence; you intimidate them with your game — that's how you intimidate them. You intimidate them with your consistency, and your opponent will fall apart—a lot of them do—when they find that you're so very consistent and that you don't give them anything for nothing.

Your training and preparation will be the source of any intimidation.

You know, I tell these kids, "You're stupid! If you make an unforced error, you have to win two points every time to get ahead of the other player. You're never gonna do it, you're not gonna do it, it's impossible! Unless the other girl or the other guy performs so badly, they miss horribly." I build confidence in the person's game; that's how I give the kid more confidence. Some people have a little more confidence than others; they're cocky. They walk out, and they're cocky; other kids have to build. Therefore, you must develop them to gain more confidence. I think the best way to make that is by having more consistency and control, and then starting to win. Playing up is probably the worst thing you can do. Playing out of your age division to avoid pressure is going to be the worst thing you can do for your kid in the long run.

19 - The Heavy Racquet

B: Tell us about how you use the weighted racquet.

R: Yes, what I do is take a racquet, and in the old days, it was straightforward, because they had these half-racquet covers that only covered the head of the racquet. Then, they started getting fancy and got these long ones that cover the whole racquet. You can improvise, by weighting a racquet. And I would have the kids use that and swing it, hit forehands and hit backhands. The reason I did it is that I had done it when I was young, at the age of 16. I started playing tennis when I was about 14, which was around 15 or 16 years old. The weather in the Netherlands was terrible, with no indoor courts available. I played for one hour a week. So, for the rest of the time, in those days, you had these wooden racquet presses that you put on top of your racquet to make it heavier. So, I go out to my room or wherever and take backhand motions for half an hour, alternating between forehand and backhand swings. I did that every day. After a while, the stroke became so grooved, and I did it perfectly; I didn't just screw around. At that point, I was really intense. My backhand follow-through was perfect (shows a complete follow-through), and my forehand follow-through was also ideal, with the arm driving and rotation. I did the perfect stroke with a heavy racquet. What happens when you put a cover on it is that it gives the resistance of the wind, and it's hard to move your wrist all over the place. You learn to control your wrist, which in turn allows you to control where the face of the racquet is, enabling you to make contact with the ball. I always recommend it to all my students, but hardly anybody follows through. They think it's a Mickey Mouse thing to do, like it's not gonna help, so they don't do it.

Weighted Frames help you develop a great follow-through

* * *

If you're ten years old and you do it for four years, your strokes would be 200% better, and your strength would be 200% better because you get so much stronger; you don't have to go to the gym and lift weights. Using a heavy racquet is one of the most effective ways to develop your shoulder strength and enhance your drive. Not many people, and not many kids, do it anymore, but I think you do it if you have some extra time; that's what you do. I mean, you wanna watch television, watch television, and swing that racquet. Do something, but swing. Make the motion, make the forehand and backhand motion.

B: Is that kind of training a core principle?

R: Well, that's precisely what it is, and it becomes automatic for the player. You drive a backhand with a bit of weight on it, and you swing through it. Forehand with a little weight on it, you swing through it. You do that often enough, you don't think about it anymore. You drive it naturally without thinking about it. I think those things are just crucial. I mean, I believe in repetition, repetition, repetition. That's what I'm a firm believer in, and as you see, I'm sort of an old soldier, and old soldiers never die, they fade away. That's what I feel like: I'm fading away. So, what happens is that all that kind of stuff is no longer considered kosher. It all has to be playing points, playing points, everybody's playing points, and all that kind of stuff. Hit the same freaking ball 200 times, that's what I believe in. Repeat, repeat, repeat. If you repeat the good stuff and eliminate the bad stuff, you're going to be great. If you allow yourself to have 100 balls and 50 bad ones, it doesn't help you. So you repeat the good stuff in everything. You figure out what you do on the good stuff; I always tell them, "figure out what you did. Why did it feel so good? What did you do? You prepared early. What happened when you followed through? Why did that ball feel so good?" Now, try to copy that and repeat it: repetition, repetition, repetition.

20 - The Mental Game

I tell my players, "If you are going to gag in the match, feel terrible the whole time you are playing, play poorly and lose. You might as well go up to the opponent at the beginning, hand them the balls, shake hands and say, 'I'm not up to it today, so here are the balls, I'm giving you the match."

21 - On Court Coaching

B: Obviously high school and college players are helped by on court coaching, but what are your thoughts about on court coaching at the pro-level?

R: I think it's a waste of time. I think it's a common thing where they thought that maybe the public would be more interested in it. They didn't really think, "Oh, would it help the player?" They thought it might help some players and possibly prolong the match to make it more interesting. First of all, 80% or less of the United States population learns how to speak foreign languages, and since they don't, 80% of foreign players; you don't really know what they're saying. I mean, they're talking some... with Wozniak, I don't know what the guy's saying in Danish. Whatever you're saying is not helping anyway. You could speak ..., maybe it would help. So I don't think it's beneficial, it's an interesting kind of thing to me because you get to play like Serena and Serena never asks her guy cuz maybe she doesn't like her guy or maybe his English has too much of a French accent or something—I have no clue—OR perhaps she has so much confidence that she knows what to do that she doesn't need him on the court. And she doesn't want to have the B.S. of asking him on the court. Like Maria asking to have someone come on the court, she doesn't even listen to the person who comes on the court; she looks up at the sky. She probably thinks, "shut up, man. I know what I'm gonna do." Anyway, it doesn't help at all.

Davenport was coaching Madison Keyes for a very short time, and Davenport is sitting in the stands, coaching, while Madison Keyes is playing like only Madison Keyes can play: either great or entirely forgetful about where the ball is going. And so, going to the third set, she calls Davenport onto the court. Up to that point, Davenport is just twisting and turning, being a nervous coach, like, 'What the hell is my player doing?' Okay? So she comes on the court and she tells Madison Keyes exactly what to do, you know, take a little more time, don't put a shot too early, you know, put a little pressure on her; but just perfect, perfect stuff to tell. Maybe it was a little on the long side, but hey, it wasn't Paul Annacone, okay? Paul Annacone gets on the court, whoever he was with, Sloane Stevens, and it's like he's reading the Bible to her. I mean, you know, that guy is on the court for like ten minutes giving Sloane Stevens so much information, Stevens didn't know what the hell was going on. So, anyway, Davenport gives Madison Keyes good advice, and she goes and sits down in the stands. First ball Madison Keyes hits, she rips the shit out of it and hits it about twenty feet wide. And it's just, I think to myself, "Oh my God!" And so, of course, Madison Keyes loses, and so I texted Davenport, I said, "Now you know what it feels like to be a coach because we all feel that we are the problem when our players lose. Like it must be our fault that the player loses, that's how we are perceived. It's never like the players are so d*** stupid, you know, it's always the coach... But you did a perfect job. You did everything right, everything was perfect, and don't let it bother you," I said, "because she was in such a mindset, ..." That's what I think happens. If there's such a mindset that it's tough to change whatever they're doing. I don't care what it is; you could tell Maria to do something, but it's just not happening. I mean, Michael Joyce was a smart guy, told her to eat a banana. I think that's the best advice he ever gave her in his whole career, you know, is to have a banana. And so I was asked to be an on-court coach years ago. I was in the desert, and so I watched my girl play, and she was playing great. She won the first set 6-2 or 6-3 against a seeded player, taking the ball early and making no errors. She wanted some advice, so I told her to keep doing what she was doing, it was working, but then she completely melted down and lost in three sets. So, I'm not a believer in on-court coaching at the pro level.

22 - Miniature Tennis

POSTED ON AUGUST 22, 2013

I am getting back into miniature tennis for the 10s and under category. I disagreed with one of the more well-known coaches in Florida. He thinks that this miniature tennis is fine. It is wrong for the very talented kids, seven and older. Can you imagine Maria Sharapova, Anna Kournikova, Pete Sampras, Monica Seles, and the Williams sisters? Yeah, the Williams sisters. Richard Williams would have gone nuts. Agassi's dad would have challenged them by boxing, such as against Stephan Edberg, Rod Laver, or the great Lew Hoad, a truly remarkable man, or my friend Pancho Segura, and forced them to play miniature tennis. Let's not forget Tracy Austin, who was great at seven on regular courts. Chris Evert, Jimmy Connors, John McEnroe, Lindsay Davenport, and Nadal or Noah, champions, were also great and very competitive at the age of 6. And let me say again, very competitive. Can you imagine John McEnroe being forced to play miniature tennis? He probably would have broken his baby racket in no time and would have been cursing in baby talk. It's great to have little 3-, 4-, 5-, and maybe 6-year-olds involved. BUT THAT IS IT !! Patrick McEnroe would have done great in miniature tennis. I also feel that it is a money maker for some people, which is why it is being pushed down the throats of these little ones. It is always the money. I sometimes hear that Hennin played miniature tennis, but I have never heard any details about it. Like when she was 4 for several months, or what? I hope professionals will organize their own tournaments for the young ones, so that the little ones can compete. You don't need the USTA. What are they going to do for any Junior younger than 14? Sending them to Spain to learn how to speak Spanish?? Nothing, but screw them up and then steal them from the pro who got them there. One of these days, I will tell you what happened to Nick Saviano. It was unreal!

23 - Maria's Coach Choices

POSTED ON JULY 31, 2013

WHAT DO I THINK OF MARIA HIRING CONNORS AS HER COACH? Maybe Maria had a brain freeze or became desperate. Maria is already the toughest player on the tour. Connors is not going to help her there. He does not know how to improve her ground game, and that is where her problem is, besides her serve. Is he going to have her charge the net more? That's like asking a bull to give milk. You can wait forever, ain't going to happen. I know exactly what has happened to her game in the last couple of years, even with Hoghstedt. But I will wait for my advice. Let's just see what Jimbo is going to come up with. We won't have to wait that long..

Knowing Maria so well, she is going to run the show. In my opinion, Maria would have been better off getting Lindsay Davenport to help her. They had the same game & Lindsay could help Maria with her serve.

I said I had the same game, because Maria is not hitting the ball the same way when she was with me. She was hitting the ball harder than anybody then. "They" probably told her to be more consistent & hit with more top spin. So wrong! That's not Maria's game, nor was it Davenport's. As soon as Lindsay dropped her pace, she would lose. She was able to put more power in her game. Seles was the same, but a better athlete than Maria, just a little!

Maria's game is simple. More power & control over the opponent. Now, a lot of people are hitting the ball harder than Maria even on the backhand. That is amazing how the game has changed, and other players catch up to you.

Maria would never miss backhands. Maria is 6' and is too slow and not athletic enough to play without pace. So Maria, go back to hitting the ball & do not toss the ball too high on your serve, it looks like you want to toss the ball to the sweet lord or whoever. You are losing too much rhythm.

Editor's Note: Michael Joyce, another Lansdorp disciple, later coached Maria.

23 - Learning To Win

Q. How should we approaching winning and losing?

A. First of all, I don't see how you can learn how to win by losing. That is not how it works. Great players hate to lose, for whatever reason, and as a result, they refuse to fail and strive hard to win. Maybe the only thing you can learn from losing is what you have to work on to get better. Hating to lose is a part of that.

Playing up without the results to back it up is a bad idea. I want to emphasize strongly how bad an idea it is! Just don't do it. If you dominate your age group and have no more competition, you can play up, but you must continue to dominate your age group. Many parents encourage their kids to play up because there is less pressure. If you can't handle the pressure, play a team sport. On a team, you can blame your teammates. I see this a lot in local league ladies playing doubles, and they always blame their partner. It seems every time they lose, it's not their fault.

You can't run away from pressure; you have to learn how to cope with it. If they lose all the time, they are bound to lose self-esteem. Girls will find a boyfriend, and boys will find a different sport or maybe a girlfriend. The tough kids will find ways to improve. Maybe get in better shape. Most kids are in lousy shape, so that's where you can improve, or become more consistent by practicing more, and become more focused and take lessons. However, in short, some kids are just incredibly resilient and will fight for every point. Just remember my motto: Consistency, Placement, Power. So if you are losing a lot, do Something about it and don't sit there and cry.

24 - No Arms, No Problem

I want your kids to go on the internet and look up "man without arms playing table tennis." Please look at this fellow and then think about yourself. You will realize real fast how unbelievably SPOILED you are and how you are not determined at all to succeed. All you kids do is complain about everything when things become just a little harder. You don't want to run down balls, oh, that is too much work. My Lord, you think to yourself, "I might sweat, I could get a little winded. And I have to keep the ball in the court and not make errors". Please, don't ask for that Much! "Goodness, this kid is moonballing me, and I can't handle all this; it's too taxing on my brain!" Then you look at you this guy, without arms, WITHOUT ARMS!, and he just can't wait to; I want to play table tennis!!!

You, the parent, are probably thinking, "Is this guy crazy?" Table tennis without arms? My kid has two good arms, two great legs, and a fine body, and takes after my wife, who has brains, and my kid can't keep more than three balls in this huge court. This man, without arms, is doing it on a table —a table, mind you. How did this man start playing table tennis? He said You know I'm going to put this paddle in my mouth and I am going to play table tennis. But how in the world am I going to serve? Simple, I am going to learn to kick the ping pong ball up in the air with my bare foot, and serve. This man is playing tournaments. The most significant difference between your kids and this man is that he is determined to make it happen.

The majority of you kids are too d*** lazy and don't want to work for anything. Your parents are probably carrying your tennis bags and pampering you before a match. Oh, of course, they don't want to upset you. What a crock. This man has discipline, and most of you don't. Why don't you kids have some of this man's determination and start working and discipline yourself? Stop complaining all the time. 90% of kids who play tennis have nothing and I mean NOTHING to whine about. You get away with complaining and feeling sorry for yourself. And if the parents think they have a talented kid, they will start pampering the kid, and now it really is over. Tracy Austin had a broken leg at the age of ten. She broke it when I accidentally fell on her leg while ice skating. Tracy would sit on a chair and hit balls every day and hit volleys. She won the US Open at the age of 16.

This man, whatever his name is, is my hero.

25 - The Carpenter

This is a true story I want parents—especially tennis parents—to read. We don't always focus on the good things our children do; often, we zero in on their mistakes and dwell too much on the negative. This can create distance between parent and child, particularly as children grow older and become more vocal.

There was once a carpenter—not Jesus—who crafted beautiful wooden cabinets, each custom-made for people in the city. He worked very hard to make them perfect. Whenever possible, he took his four-year-old son to work with him. The little boy would watch his father intently. One day, the father was nearly finished with a cabinet he'd spent weeks creating. Just before he was to deliver it, he stepped away for a moment. When he returned, he found his son had hammered nails into the beautiful cabinet. The father looked at his son and said, "That's a beautiful job, my son. Thank you so much for helping Daddy." He then carefully removed the nails and repaired the cabinet. It took time, but everything turned out fine.

This story makes me reflect on how I could handle similar situations. The love between a parent and child truly is one of life's most beautiful things.

26 - Building Fundamentals and Adaptability

My philosophy isn't about chasing trends or copying the latest pro on TV. It's about building a foundation that lasts, one that blends discipline, consistency, and power with the flexibility to adapt to each player's unique strengths. All of my top players have had strokes that look different from each other; the core of my teaching remains the same: attitude, fundamentals, and an unrelenting focus on hitting the ball right. Let me take you through what that means for you—whether you're a player or a coach—and how to apply it on the court.

The Core of My Teaching:
Same Attitude, Different Strokes

When I step onto the court with a player, whether they're 8 years old or 18, my approach starts with mindset. I teach every player the same way when it comes to attitude: show up, work hard, stay disciplined, and commit to consistency. That's non-negotiable. You can have the prettiest forehand in the world, but if you're not mentally locked in, it's worthless. I tell my players, "Tennis is a fight. You're not just hitting a ball—you're battling your opponent, your nerves, and sometimes yourself." That's the foundation. Where people get it wrong: they think I cookie-cut every player's strokes to look identical. Not true. I adapt to the player. Take two kids I coach—a 10-year-old girl and her 8-year-old brother. Their dad, a former player himself, once told me he's amazed at how I say just the right thing to each kid, tailored to their personality and game. The girl needs confidence to drive the ball; the boy needs to focus on timing. Their strokes? Not identical. But the principles—power, precision, and consistency —are the same. In the 1970s, teaching was simpler. Grips were straightforward, and the game was less about extreme spin. Today, with modern rackets and strings, players lean toward heavy topspin and western grips. That's fine, but I don't let my players get stuck in one gear. I teach what I call the "academy ball"—a high, spinny shot that clears the net by four or five feet. It's safe, consistent, and perfect for kids' learning control. The catch in all this is, if you only hit that kind of ball, you'll plateau by 14. You've got to learn to drive the ball harder, lower, and with purpose. That's where champions separate themselves.

Fundamentals First: The Sound of a Clean Hit

When I watch a player, I don't just look at their form—I listen. The sound of the ball coming off the racket tells me everything. A clean, solid hit—smack in the center of the strings—has a distinct pop. It's crisp, like a drumbeat. That's what I want my players to chase. Timing, contact point, and racket face angle have to align perfectly for that sound. When I hear it, I know the ball's coming off right—whether it's a forehand, backhand, or serve.For coaches, this is critical: train your ear as much as your eye. A player might look like they're swinging correctly, but if the ball sounds mushy or off, something's wrong. Maybe their grip's slipping, or they're not meeting the ball cleanly. Fix it early. For players, focus on that contact point. Feel the ball hit the sweet spot. That's your feedback loop, not some fancy video analysis. My fundamentals haven't changed much since I started coaching. On the forehand, I want a solid base, weight transfer, and a natural follow-through, not exaggerated. I'm not a fan of the extreme topspin forehand with a windshield-wiper finish—it's too hard to control under pressure. On the backhand, I prefer a flatter shot, maybe with a touch of topspin for safety. Extreme topspin backhands? They're inconsistent for most players, especially kids. Keep it simple, keep it solid.

The Grip Conundrum: Adapt, Don't Overcomplicate

Grips are where things get tricky today. Back in the day, eastern or continental grips ruled. Now, kids show up with semi-western or full-western grips, chasing Nadal's spin. I don't fight it entirely—I'll work with a western grip if that's what they've got. But here's the problem: if a kid's grip slides too extreme, it's a trap. Once they're locked into a full western grip, it's nearly impossible to flatten out their shots. And trust me, you need to hit flat sometimes to attack effectively. For young players, I start with a semi-western grip for the forehand. It gives you enough spin to keep the ball in but lets you drive it when needed. If a kid's grip starts creeping too extreme, I'll adjust it early—say, at 7 or 8 years old—before it's cemented. Coaches, watch those grips like a hawk. A kid might hit a great "academy ball" with tons of spin, but if their grip's too extreme, they'll struggle to add pace or vary their shots later. Players, don't get seduced by spin. Spin's a tool, not your whole game.

Height Over the Net: Striking the Balance

One of the biggest debates I hear is about how high the ball should clear the net. Some coaches swear by the "six feet over the net" rule, pointing to pros like Nadal or Djokovic. Let me set this straight: TV graphics are misleading. Every shot looks like it's arcing high, even a flat drive or a slice. Don't trust the screen—trust the court. My rule? If you can consistently clear the net by 2.5 to 3 feet, you're in business. That's the sweet spot for aggressive, controlled tennis. You can mix in higher, spinnier shots to change pace or defend, but if every ball's soaring five or six feet over, you're giving your opponent too much time. Look at Kim Clijsters—her drives cleared about 2.5 feet on average, and she was a champion. Even top men mix their heights, but their bread-and-butter shots aren't looping moonballs.

For young players, start with the academy ball—higher, spinnier, safer. It builds confidence and keeps rallies going. But by 7 or 8, I'm pushing them to hit harder and lower. Take the 10-year-old girl I coach. She hits a beautiful, deep academy ball, four feet over the net. It's consistent, and she can outlast bigger girls. But against aggressive players who crank the ball, she's in trouble unless she learns to drive it lower and harder. Coaches, don't let your players get comfortable with just one shot. Players, challenge yourself to take the ball earlier and flatten it out. You'll thank me when you're facing a pusher who eats high balls for breakfast.

When to Push the Gas: Building Power Early

I start pushing players to hit harder by the time they're 7 or 8 years old. That might sound young, but it's critical. In the U.S., we excel at teaching control but struggle with teaching power. You can always take pace off a shot, but adding it later? That's tough. Kids get stuck in a defensive mindset, looping balls deep and safe. That works in juniors, but it won't cut it against elite players. Balance is key. Teach kids to hit hard and low, but give them the spin option for defense. By their teens, they should have both gears.

Final Thoughts for Players and Coaches

My philosophy boils down to this: build a game that's versatile, disciplined, and aggressive. Don't chase fads—extreme grips, moonball topspin, or whatever's trending on TV. Focus on fundamentals: a clean hit, a solid base, and a mindset that refuses to quit. Coaches, tailor your teaching to the player's strengths, but don't compromise on attitude or consistency. Players, listen to the sound of your shots, feel the ball off your strings, and push yourself to hit with purpose. Tennis has changed since I started, but the path to greatness hasn't. It's about mastering the basics, adapting to the player, and building a game that can win on any court, against any opponent. That's my way!

27 - Evaluating Talent: Timing And Instinctiveness

When I step onto a court with a new player, I'm not looking for the flashiest swing or the biggest muscles. I'm watching for something deeper, something that separates the good from the great: timing. Over the course of my decades coaching players like Pete Sampras, Lindsay Davenport, and Maria Sharapova, I've learned that timing is the heartbeat of tennis. It's not just about hitting the ball—it's about when and how you hit it. For players and coaches, understanding this is the key to unlocking potential. Let me break down what I look for when evaluating a player's physical talent and how to build a game that can climb to the top.

Timing: The Foundation of Greatness.

Timing is everything in tennis, yet it is often the most overlooked aspect of the game. I don't care how strong or fast a player is—if they can't time the ball, they're capped. Great players, from Sampras to Davenport, had an innate sense of when to meet the ball. It's not just about speed; it's about precision. The ball has to hit the sweet spot of the racket, producing that crisp, clean pop. When I evaluate a player, I watch their contact point. Are they hitting the ball out in front, or are they late, dragging the racket through? That split-second difference tells me their ceiling.Take Maria Sharapova. Her backhand timing was phenomenal—sharp, controlled, deadly. But her forehand? Lousy from day one. She hit it late, almost like she was using a continental grip from the 1970s, when players could afford to be tardy with their contact. Modern grips —semi-western or western—demand an earlier hit to control the ball's spin and direction. Maria's late forehand meant she often had only one option: down the line. It was a flat, powerful shot, but it limited her versatility. She became a champion despite this flaw, which speaks volumes about her determination and perseverance. But it's also a lesson: timing flaws can hold you back, even if you're world-class.Coaches, train your eye to spot timing. Watch where the ball meets the racket. Listen for the sound—a clean hit sounds different from a mishit. Players, focus on meeting the ball out in front, not chasing it. Timing isn't just mechanics; it's about vision and anticipation. I've heard coaches talk about eye dominance—how a stronger right eye might make a player late on the forehand—but I don't get hung up on science. I go by feel. If a kid's consistently late, I adjust their stance, grip, or preparation to get them hitting earlier. It's instinct, not a lab experiment.

The Grip Factor: Adapting to Modern Tennis Grips Has Changed the Game, and They Affect Timing More Than Most Coaches Realize.

In the past, continental grips allowed players to hit the ball late and still maintain control. Think of it like driving a stick-shift car—forgiving, but limited. Modern western or semi-western grips are like automatic transmissions: they demand precision and early contact to harness spin and power. When I see a kid with an extreme grip hitting flat, down-the-line forehands, I know they're in trouble. They've trained one shot at the expense of versatility, like Maria's forehand stuck in one gear.With Maria, I worked on reverse forehands to compensate. A reverse forehand—where the racket face opens slightly to guide the ball crosscourt—forces earlier timing and better racket face control. Pete Sampras didn't need it as much; his timing was so natural he could hit any shot, any direction, with ease. Lindsay Davenport, too, had impeccable timing, letting her rip controlled, powerful shots off both wings. Coaches, don't let your players fall into the trap of one-dimensional shots. Teach them to vary their angles—crosscourt, down the line, inside-out—by adjusting their contact point and racket face. Players, practice hitting earlier, especially if you're using a modern grip. It's the difference between being predictable and being unstoppable.

Beyond Timing: What I Look For

Timing is my starting point, but I also evaluate movement and coordination. A player doesn't need to be a sprinter, but they need to move efficiently—low center of gravity, quick feet, balanced recovery. I watch how a kid glides to the ball. Are they clunky or fluid? Do they recover after a shot or stumble? Pete moved like a cat, always ready for the next ball. Lindsay had a big frame but was smooth and deliberate. Maria's intensity made up for less natural movement, but she worked at it. Coaches, drill footwork relentlessly—lateral shuffles, split steps, recovery steps. Players, treat movement like a skill, not an afterthought. You can't time the ball if you're not in position.I also look at a player's eyes—not just for tracking but for focus. A great player locks onto the ball like a hawk. It's not just vision; it's intent. Tracy Austin, at 7, had that stare—intense, unyielding. It told me she was coachable and hungry. Coaches, take note of your players' demeanor. Are they dialed in or distracted? Players, train your focus as much as your forehand. Watch the ball from your opponent's racket to yours, every time.

Avoiding Overcomplication: Keep It Natural.

I don't mess with angles or degrees—none of that "45-degree contact point" nonsense. That's for scientists, not coaches. If I told a kid to hit at a 45-degree angle, they'd freeze, overthinking every swing. Tennis is feel, not math. I tell players to hit "out in front," where the ball feels solid and the racket face points naturally toward the target. With Maria, I'd set crosscourt targets to force her to hit earlier, opening her racket face to guide the ball rather than dragging it late. It wasn't about angles—it was about instinct and repetition. Coaches, avoid overwhelming your players with technical jargon. Teach them to feel the shot.

Set up drills that reward clean, early contact—crosscourt rallies, down-the-line challenges, or targets just beyond the net. Players, trust your body's instincts. If you're thinking about degrees or swing paths, you're not playing tennis—you're doing geometry. Please focus on the ball, meet it cleanly, and let your racket do the talking.

The Upper Limit: Timing Meets Grit.

When evaluating a player's potential, timing is my guiding principle, but it's not the whole story. A kid might have perfect timing but lack the fight to push through tough matches. Others, like Maria, can overcome timing flaws with sheer will. The great ones—Sampras, Davenport, Austin—had both: impeccable timing and unrelenting competitiveness. A player with great timing but no heart might reach the top 20. Add grit, and they're contending for number one. Coaches, your job is to test both. Push your players with tough drills to see how they respond. Do they crumble or fight? Players, timing is your foundation, but your mentality builds the house. Work on meeting the ball cleanly, but also train your mind to stay tough when the score's tight. That's what separates the good from the great.

The Lansdorp Way: Instinct and Simplicity.

My approach to evaluating talent hasn't changed in decades. I don't need fancy metrics or videos breaking down Maria's hip rotation. I watch, I listen, I feel. Timing, movement, focus—these are the pillars. Build them early, and you're building a player who can go the distance. Please keep it simple, trust your instincts, and teach your players to fight for every ball. That's how you find—and shape—a champion.

28 - A Letter To Robert On Tournament Play

Coach Lansdorp,

Thank you for taking the time to express your thoughts on the critical issues before us and the tennis community. I sincerely appreciate your knowledge and insights and have the greatest respect for your leadership and accomplishments. With some luck and much persistence, perhaps we can jointly undo the gimmickry and ill conceived dogmas that the USTA has offered to the tennis community as, in their view, a well conceived prescription for the development of champions.

Best Regards,

***

Mr. B****, I read your articles with interest. I want you to understand that it is not necessary that Champions are developed by USTA or ITF tournaments in later years. After all, a Champion, the way I describe a Champion, is already playing PRO tournaments at the age of 16, especially girls. Boys may be one year later. Maria Sharapova won Wimbledon at 17 and hardly played Junior tournaments. NO USTA tournaments. Sampras won the U.S. Open at the age of 19 and was playing pro tournaments at 16. Played lots of USTA tournaments at a young age. Forget Tracy Austin, she was a joke, so good. She won the US Open at 16 and was playing lots of USTA tournaments at a very young age, and thank god they did not have miniature tennis in those days. Lindsay Davenport won the Swiss open, CLAY, at the age of 16. Michael Chang won the French at barely 17, but played a lot of junior tournaments at a very young age. So did every Champion. What I am getting at is that tournaments are great for kids. The more tournaments they can play, the better. It is a great way to become a very good player, to develop as a person and get an excellent scholarship. Something that over 90 percent of juniors should have a chance to experience. HOWEVER, if you are an 18-year-old girl and are not doing well on the Pro tour, the opportunity to become a Champion is slim. If you are an 18-year-old boy, you have the same problem. That's why you should not have your very talented kids play miniature tennis, but have them play regular tennis. The beginning years are crucial in the development of the kid in what ever they do. That is where the USTA Junior Development is failing. Currently (2013), they are not interested in the early years of development. Remember, the younger years are CRUCIAL. The USTA does not understand this. They come up with gimmicks, like miniature tennis. Great for thousands of little 4, 5, and 6-year-olds. So tournaments are great. Have these kids compete, regardless of their age, whether they are 10 or 18. Don't make the tournaments small; make them large. The few gifted Juniors are not playing the 18's and under when they are 18, maybe when they are 14. But don't take it away from all the other juniors. Europe has tons of Satellite and Challenger tournaments. I agree with you 100%.

29 - On USTA Player Development

Why does the USTA Junior Development not understand that they will never develop a champion and that THAT is really not their job!? The USTA should be a SUPPORTING organization, NOTHING MORE, NOTHING LESS. The most difficult, and most important years of development are between the ages of 6 or 7 till about 15 for girls and 16 for boys. It is a very taxing time for developing youngsters. Their DISCIPLINE, their FOCUS, their CONSISTENCY in their behavior and their tennis, their DESIRE TO WIN, loving to COMPETE, their LOVE to WORK HARD, NOT playing to lose, but the desire to WIN, CONDITIONING themselves, becoming INDEPENDENT THINKERS, and working on the RIGHT TECHNIQUE. The beginning years are hugely important in the development of the child. When it comes to the TECHNIQUE, it is crucial. You can ruin a kid in the first couple of years. I have only touched a small part, BUT you can see that the USTA is not interested in doing that real development. First of all, they don't know what to do, but they lack the time and desire to do so. Then, after coaches have worked their butts off, the USTA will come around and basically steal the student, instead of involving the coach or parent in the further development of the junior. Instead of asking the coach who has worked with the kid, how can they help? Don't take the kid away from the environment that created them. Many coaches offer extra time and sometimes financial assistance to help their students grow, and they take pride in their accomplishments, only to have the USTA "take" the kid, hoping to deceive people into thinking the USTA did the job. Another thing. When somebody makes it on the tour and makes great money, WHY does the USTA pay for their coaching, travel, and coaches' expenses? Why, so they can claim to be affiliated with the USTA and receive coaching from them. Have them pay their own expenses, like everybody else. After all, if the USTA is that great, they will be willing to pay top dollar for your coaching and use that money to help needy juniors.

30 - Coaches, Parents and Parent/Coaches

POSTED ON AUGUST 18, 2013

Who Is The Biggest Problem?

OMG, now it is the parents. It is NOT the parents. IT IS THE COACHING. Most coaches in this country have limited knowledge of effective coaching techniques. They are just horrible. They know how to talk a great game, and people believe them. You don't know who is excellent and who is not. The teaching organizations are now focused on quantity, rather than quality. Anybody is a coach these days. If you can poke a ball over the net and get a basket of balls, you are a coach. If you can talk a great game, you must be great. So many times, the parents are smarter than the "pro" and know more. But it is not the parents!

Tennis Academies

Another thing happening in this country is that everybody has academies! Academies don't create Champions. They don't, not at the highest levels. People don't want to believe me. Every club in the US has an academy, or if the coach has one pretty good player, he will start an "academy " for more money in his pocket. So, the one-on-one has left this country. Name one top 10 tennis player who has come out of the Chris Evert academy in the last 10 years. Name me one—even a top 30 player. I like Rick Macci, but who has come out of his academy in the last decade? And all these so, so academies in clubs don't develop players. If in the past the kids were in academies, it was always a family member running the show. They were in control.

I am at fault a little. My rates have increased to $200 per hour. Not outrageous, like some pros, but too expensive for many people. So, the one-on-one is disappearing. "Academies" are popping up all over the place, and now comes the second problem. Everybody, and I mean everybody, is hitting lots of topspin and hitting academy balls. High over the net with lots of topspin. Then you look at the top pros, and they are all hitting the ball extremely hard. Very hard, relatively low over the net, not much higher than 2 1/2 feet over the net consistently well. Consistent, because they have been doing it since they were young. This academy ball is a significant issue in producing champions. Because of the academies, you are losing the one-on-one teaching, and discipline suffers as a result. Now you are in real trouble. No discipline.... no champions. Additionally, the attitude of people has changed since the Capriati debacle. Let's go to college. Nothing wrong with that, but no champion will develop with that attitude. And don't bring up Isner. About 99% of world-class players didn't attend high school and never went to college. Combining the two does not work. Attending a tough private High School is essentially the end of becoming a great player; forget about becoming a champion. On top of all this, you have a bunch of money-hungry people running the USTA junior "development" program. Nothing good will come out of the USTA junior development. Just poaching players from other coaches, only to mess them up and forget them. What a great organization. There are hundreds of very talented youngsters in this country, but they don't develop into champions. Making champions is an art and a gift.

Editor's Note: Robert's comments here are 12 years old, and in recent years, more players have made the jump from college to making the top 100 in the world, but there has not been a college player who has been #1 in the world for quite some time, and few in the top 10.

Appendix A - Robert's Top Drills

Robert Lansdorp's coaching drills were renowned for their intensity, simplicity, and focus on building technically sound, powerful groundstrokes, particularly the flat, penetrating "Lansdorp Forehand" and backhand, designed to skim low over the net (2-2.5 feet) for aggressive play. His methods emphasized repetition, precision, and mental toughness over innate talent, shaped by his belief that disciplined practice forged champions. Below is a detailed breakdown of his key drills and coaching techniques, drawn from available sources.

Signature Drills

"20 at the Baseline" Drill

Description: Players had to hit 20 consecutive groundstrokes (forehands or backhands) in bounds without a single miss. If a shot went out, the count reset to zero, forcing relentless focus and consistency.

Purpose: Built accuracy, endurance, and mental discipline under pressure. Lansdorp believed missing shots in practice translated to errors in matches.

Execution: Conducted during one-on-one sessions, often with Lansdorp feeding balls from a supermarket cart filled with hundreds of tennis balls, ensuring continuous rallies for up to an hour.

Impact: Players like Tracy Austin and Pete Sampras credited this drill for their ability to sustain long rallies and hit precise, aggressive shots in high-stakes moments. Austin noted it instilled a "no-mistake" mindset.

Tennis Can on Broom Handle Drill

Description: A tennis can was placed on a broom handle at the net, serving as a target. Players had to hit groundstrokes to knock the can off repeatedly.

Purpose: Developed pinpoint accuracy and control over shot trajectory, reinforcing Lansdorp's low-net-clearance philosophy.

It also trained players to aim for specific court zones.

Execution: Lansdorp would set up the target and feed balls, demanding players hit the can consistently. Missing required restarting, adding pressure to perform.

Impact: This drill helped players like Maria Sharapova refine their forehand consistency and Lindsay Davenport develop her powerful, flat groundstrokes.

Supermarket Cart Feeding

Description: Lansdorp used a large supermarket cart filled with 300-400 tennis balls to feed continuous shots during lessons, minimizing downtime and maximizing repetitions.

Purpose: Ensured high-volume practice to groove muscle memory for groundstrokes. The sheer number of balls allowed for extended rallies, simulating match-like endurance.

Execution: He fed balls at varying speeds and angles, challenging players to adjust footwork and stroke mechanics on the fly. Sessions could last an hour or more, often exhausting players.

Impact: This relentless approach built the stamina and technical precision seen in players like Sampras, whose running forehand became a weapon, and Davenport, known for her relentless baseline game.

Crosscourt and Down-the-Line Drills

Description: Players hit alternating crosscourt and down-the-line groundstrokes, focusing on specific targets (e.g., corners of the court) to develop versatility and placement.

Purpose: Trained players to control shot direction and depth while maintaining the flat, low trajectory Lansdorp favored. It also improved footwork and court coverage.

Execution: Lansdorp fed balls to force players to move laterally, hitting forehands and backhands to designated zones. Errors reset the drill, reinforcing consistency.

Impact: Eliot Teltscher's pure one-handed backhand and Sharapova's improved forehand consistency were honed through these drills, enabling them to dictate points.

***
Coaching Techniques and Philosophy

Repetition Over Talent: Lansdorp believed talent was secondary to disciplined practice. He drilled players to hit thousands of balls to perfect technique, often saying, "You don't have to be talented to be great; you have to work." This was evident in his work with young players like Austin (starting at age 7) and Sampras (age 10), whose groundstrokes became world-class through repetition.

Focus on Groundstrokes: His drills prioritized flat, aggressive forehands and backhands over topspin-heavy "academy ball," which he criticized as ineffective for top-level play. He taught a "buggy whip" forehand motion—early preparation, full extension, and a follow-through wrapping around the body—to generate power and control.

Mental Toughness: Drills were designed to be grueling, testing players' resilience. Resetting counts after misses forced players to overcome frustration, mirroring match pressure. His intimidating presence (6'3", stern demeanor) pushed players like Austin to develop fearlessness.

Individualized Approach: Lansdorp tailored drills to each player's needs. For Sampras, he emphasized the running forehand; for Sharapova, he refined her forehand for consistency; for Davenport, he focused on power and depth. He avoided academies, preferring one-on-one sessions on public or private courts for personalized attention.

Live Ball Drills: Unlike static ball-machine drills, Lansdorp fed "live" balls by hand, varying spin, speed, and placement to simulate real match conditions. This forced players to adapt dynamically, improving reaction time and footwork.

Specific Examples with Players

Tracy Austin: Starting at age 7, Austin endured the "20 at the baseline" drill, which built her flawless groundstrokes, leading to her 1979 US Open title at 16. Lansdorp's repetitive drills gave her the consistency to outlast opponents.

Pete Sampras: From age 10, Sampras worked on his running

forehand through crosscourt/down-the-line drills, making it a signature shot. Lansdorp's cart-feeding sessions built his endurance for long baseline rallies.

Lindsay Davenport: Lansdorp's drills from age 9 focused on power, using the tennis can drill to refine her flat, deep groundstrokes. Her ability to hit winners from the baseline stemmed from these sessions.

Maria Sharapova: Lansdorp refined her forehand for consistency using repetitive crosscourt drills, helping her maintain control during aggressive play. The "20 at the baseline" drill sharpened her precision.

Environment and Style

Lansdorp conducted drills on public courts like Morley Field or private facilities like the Jack Kramer Club, avoiding the structured academy model. His sessions were intense, often lasting hours, with minimal breaks to mimic match stamina. He used verbal cues and demonstrations to correct form, emphasizing early racket preparation and weight transfer. His gruff, no-nonsense demeanor—sometimes yelling to push players—created a high-pressure environment that prepared them for compete.

Legacy of Drills

Lansdorp's drills produced 24 Grand Slam titles across his pupils, with four reaching world No. 1. His focus on repetition and precision influenced modern baseline-heavy play, and his methods were praised by players like Austin, who called him the best groundstroke coach ever, and Teltscher, who said his drills built not just technique but character. His daughter Stephanie continued his legacy, applying similar drills at West End Tennis Club.

These drills, rooted in simplicity and discipline, transformed raw talent into championship-level skill, cementing Lansdorp's reputation as a legendary coach.

Appendix B - 7 Traits Of Robert's Coaching

Robert Lansdorp's coaching techniques were innovative in tennis, and many of his new paradigms have been adopted by the mainstream coaching community. He produced four world No. 1 players—Tracy Austin, Pete Sampras, Lindsay Davenport, and Maria Sharapova—who collectively won 24 Grand Slam titles, alongside over 20 top-20 and 50 top-100 professionals. His genius lay in a blend of technical precision, relentless repetition, psychological conditioning, and individualized instruction, all rooted in a philosophy that prioritized discipline over talent. Below is a detailed analysis of the key elements that made his methods exceptional, grounded in his approach and results.

1. Technical Mastery: The "Lansdorp Forehand" and Low, Flat Groundstrokes

Genius: Lansdorp's signature contribution was his emphasis on flat, penetrating groundstrokes that skimmed the net (2-2.5 feet clearance), known as the "Lansdorp Forehand" or "buggy whip forehand." Unlike the topspin-heavy "academy ball" prevalent in junior programs, his shots were aggressive, low-trajectory, and designed to dominate points by reducing opponents' reaction time.

Mechanics: He taught early racket preparation, full extension, and a follow-through wrapping around the body, maximizing power and control. This technique required precise timing and footwork, which he drilled relentlessly.

Impact: Players like Pete Sampras developed a devastating running forehand, while Lindsay Davenport's flat groundstrokes became point-enders. Tracy Austin's flawless consistency at the 1979 US Open (winning at 16) stemmed from this technique, and Maria Sharapova's refined forehand consistency helped her compete at the highest levels. His rejection of high-arcing topspin anticipated the modern baseline-heavy game, making his players tactically ahead of their time.

Why Genius: By focusing on flat shots, Lansdorp gave his players an edge in an era transitioning from serve-and-volley to baseline play. His foresight in prioritizing aggressive, low-margin shots shaped champions who could dictate rallies, a hallmark of modern tennis.

2. Relentless Repetition: Building Muscle Memory Through Drills

Genius: Lansdorp's mantra, "You don't have to be talented to be great; you have to work," underpinned his use of high-volume, repetitive drills like "20 at the baseline" (hitting 20 consecutive groundstrokes without error) and the tennis can on a broom handle (targeting for accuracy). These drills ingrained muscle memory and precision under pressure.

Execution: Using a supermarket cart with 300-400 balls, he fed continuous shots for hour-long sessions, minimizing downtime. Missing a shot resets the count, forcing players to focus intensely on their next attempt. The "tennis can" drill honed pinpoint accuracy by requiring players to knock a can off a broom handle repeatedly.

Impact: This repetition built the consistency seen in Austin's error-free baseline game and Sampras's ability to hit winners on the run. Sharapova's forehand reliability and Davenport's deep, powerful shots were products of thousands of repetitions. Over 50 top-100 players emerged from this method, proving its scalability.

Why Genius: Lansdorp understood that elite performance required automating complex movements. His drills simulated match pressure, ensuring players could execute shots instinctively in high-stakes situations —a precursor to modern sports science's emphasis on deliberate practice.

3. Psychological Conditioning: Forging Mental Toughness

Genius: Lansdorp's gruff, intimidating style (6'3", stern demeanor) and demanding drills cultivated mental resilience, preparing players for the psychological rigors of professional tennis. He believed surviving frustration in practice—e.g., resetting the "20 at the baseline" drill after a miss—translated to composure in matches.

Approach: His sessions were grueling, often lasting hours with minimal breaks, mimicking match stamina. He pushed players to overcome errors without losing focus, drawing from his own childhood resilience during wartime hardships. Quotes like "If you can't handle missing 20 shots in a row and starting over, you won't handle a fifth set" reflect this ethos.

Impact: Austin's fearlessness at 16 against top players, Sampras's clutch performances in Grand Slams, and Davenport's ability to grind out long rallies all trace back to Lansdorp's mental conditioning. Eliot Teltscher noted that his influence extended beyond tennis, shaping life skills.

Why Genius: Lansdorp's ability to instill a "no-excuses" mindset was revolutionary in an era when mental coaching was less formalized. His drills doubled as psychological tests, aligning with modern sports psychology's emphasis on grit and focus.

4. Individualized Coaching: Tailoring to Each Player

Genius: Unlike academy-style coaches, Lansdorp avoided one-size-fits-all methods, preferring one-on-one sessions on public or private courts (e.g., Morley Field, Jack Kramer Club). He tailored drills to each player's strengths and weaknesses, ensuring personalized development.

Examples: For Sampras, he emphasized the running forehand to complement his serve-and-volley game. For

Sharapova, he refined her forehand for consistency. For Davenport, he focused on power and depth. For Teltscher, he perfected a pure one-handed backhand. This adaptability produced diverse champions across playing styles.

Execution: He fed "live" balls by hand, varying spin and placement to simulate match conditions, unlike static ball machines. This dynamic approach improved reaction time and adaptability, tailored to each player's needs.

Why Genius: His rejection of academies and focus on individual attention anticipated personalized coaching trends. By adapting drills to each player, he maximized their potential, producing versatile champions who thrived in different eras.

5. Pioneering Baseline Dominance

Genius: Lansdorp's focus on aggressive groundstrokes foreshadowed the shift from serve-and-volley to baseline-dominated tennis in the 1990s and beyond. His criticism of "academy ball" and the USTA's topspin-heavy junior programs showed his foresight in prioritizing power and precision.

Evidence: His players' 24 Grand Slam titles, including Austin's 1979 US Open and Sampras's 14 majors, reflect a style that became the blueprint for modern tennis. His methods influenced players like Andre Agassi indirectly through the evolution of baseline play.

Why Genius: Lansdorp's vision aligned with technological changes (e.g., larger rackets, slower courts) that favored baseline play. His techniques gave players a competitive edge, shaping the sport's tactical evolution.

6. Long-Term Relationships and Early Development

Genius: Lansdorp often started coaching players as young as 7-10 (Austin at 7, Sampras at 10, Davenport at 9), building their games from scratch. His long-term commitment fostered trust and loyalty, resulting in lifelong bonds and consistent improvement.

Impact: Starting early allowed him to ingrain his technique and mindset, as seen in Austin's rapid rise and Sampras's development into a 14-time major champion. His role as one of the first non-family traveling coaches on the women's tour (e.g., with Austin) set a precedent for dedicated coaching.

Why Genius: His ability to mold young players over decades ensured technical and mental foundations that lasted entire careers, a model now standard in elite coaching.

7. Defiance of Conventional Systems

Genius: Lansdorp's maverick status—rejecting academies and criticizing the USTA's "10 and under" program (miniature courts, green-dot balls)—allowed him to innovate freely. He believed such systems hindered talent, advocating for rigorous training on full-size courts even for juniors.

Impact: His independent approach produced unique players who stood out against academy-trained peers. His success validated his methods, earning him the USTA Lifetime Achievement Award (2005) and ITF Services to the Game Award.

Why Genius: By challenging institutional norms, Lansdorp carved a niche that prioritized results over conformity, influencing coaching philosophies beyond tennis.

Synthesis of Genius

Lansdorp's genius was in synthesizing technical innovation (flat groundstrokes), psychological rigor (challenging drills), and personalized coaching into a system that produced consistent, world-class results. His methods were both timeless—rooted in universal principles of hard work and precision—and forward-thinking, anticipating the baseline era. His ability to transform young players into champions through repetition, tailored instruction, and mental fortitude set a standard that influenced modern tennis coaching. As Tracy Austin said, he was "the best groundstroke teacher ever," a testament to his enduring impact. His legacy lives on through players, his daughter Stephanie's coaching, and the sport's evolution toward aggressive baseline play.

Appendix C 7 Quotes/Context Robert's Legacy

Robert Lansdorp was known for his direct, no-nonsense approach to coaching, and his quotes reflect his philosophy of discipline, hard work, and technical precision in tennis. Below is a compilation of notable quotes attributed to him, drawn from available sources, along with context where relevant. Note that Lansdorp's outspoken nature often led to candid, sometimes humorous remarks, though direct quotes are limited due to his preference for on-court instruction over public speaking.

On Talent vs. Hard Work:
Quote: "You don't have to be talented to be great; you have to work."
Context: Lansdorp emphasized relentless practice over innate ability, a cornerstone of his coaching. He believed his repetitive drills, like "20 at the baseline," could mold any dedicated player into a champion, as seen with pupils like Tracy Austin and Pete Sampras. This quote encapsulates his belief that discipline trumps natural talent.

On His Coaching Style:
Quote: "I'm not here to make friends; I'm here to make you better."
Context: Known for his gruff, intimidating demeanor (standing 6'3"), Lansdorp used this mindset to push players like Lindsay Davenport and Maria Sharapova to their limits. His tough-love approach during drills built mental toughness, though it could be daunting for young players.

On Groundstroke Technique:
Quote: "Hit it low, hit it hard, hit it flat—two feet over the net, no more."
Context: Lansdorp's signature "Lansdorp Forehand" and backhand focused on flat, penetrating shots that skimmed the net (2-2.5 feet clearance). He rejected high-arcing topspin shots ("academy ball"), believing his method produced aggressive, point-ending strokes, as seen in players like Austin and Davenport.

***

On the USTA's Junior Development Program:
Quote: "Miniature courts and green-dot balls? That's not how you build champions."

Context: In 2012, Lansdorp publicly criticized the USTA's "10 and under" program, which used smaller courts and low-compression balls. He argued it hindered talented kids' development, reflecting his preference for rigorous, adult-level training even for juniors.

On Player Gratitude (Humorous):
Quote: "Maria [Sharapova] still owes me a Mercedes."

Context: In a 2004 interview, Lansdorp jokingly lamented that his millionaire pupils, like Sharapova, rarely sent him gifts despite his role in their success. This reflected his candid, self-deprecating humor about his contributions to their careers.

On Mental Toughness:
Quote: "If you can't handle missing 20 shots in a row and starting over, you won't handle a fifth set."

Context: Lansdorp's "20 at the baseline" drill, where players had to hit 20 consecutive groundstrokes without error, was designed to build resilience. He believed surviving the frustration of resetting the count prepared players like Sampras for high-pressure match situations.

On His Legacy:
Quote: "I don't care about fame. I care about seeing my kids hit the ball right."

Context: Lansdorp shunned the spotlight, avoiding academies and media attention. His focus was on perfecting his players' technique, as evidenced by his work with over 20 top-20 pros. This quote, shared by a former pupil, highlights his dedication to coaching over personal recognition.

Robert's Bio

I was born Robert Herman Lansdorp on November 12, 1938, in Semarang, in the Dutch East Indies—what's now Indonesia—to Dutch parents. My father, Herman, was a Goodyear executive born right there in Indonesia, overseeing operations that kept our family in a privileged but precarious world of staff and chauffeurs. My mother, Hilda (née Skinner), managed the household with incredible fortitude; her parents were Dutch and Scottish, infusing her with a mix of stubborn resilience that she passed down to me. I had an older sister named Louise, and later a younger brother joined us. Those first years were incredibly tough, marked by dangers that could have made headlines, but I never felt bad about it afterward—it's just the way life can be sometimes. Looking back, that upbringing forged me, and I do try to give kids the opportunities I didn't have. I sometimes wonder how good I might have been as a player if I'd had myself as a coach from the start.

My earliest memory of peril came at age three, in 1941 or so, when one of the chauffeurs my dad had fired poisoned me out of revenge. It was a close call—some toxic substance slipped into my food—but I survived because, as the story goes, I was a little piglet who ate everything in sight, diluting whatever was meant to kill me. Not long after, World War II erupted, turning our world upside down. The Japanese invaded and occupied Indonesia, capturing my father and interning him in a brutal concentration camp for the duration. My mom, with us kids, had to fend for ourselves; she carried false papers claiming she was Danish to avoid worse fates, and she stuck to that story even when tortured by interrogators. The details of her suffering are harrowing—beatings, threats, isolation—but she never broke, protecting us all. I'm not going into every graphic detail now; maybe someday in full, but it was hell.

As the war ended in 1945, Indonesia's push for independence from Dutch colonial rule ignited fresh violence against expatriates like us. Dutch families, fearing for their lives, banded together in an emptied-out Japanese concentration camp for safety in numbers—though we had no real armed protection. I was about six or seven then. One terrifying night, Indonesian fighters attacked one section of the camp, massacring hundreds of Dutch men, women, and children in a bloodbath. We huddled in our area, waiting for what seemed inevitable, when suddenly an English patrol—God bless them—arrived and liberated us just in time. Hooray for the English! They evacuated us in rattling trucks and creaky old ships, bouncing us from Middle Java to West Java, and finally to the capital, Batavia (later renamed Jakarta).

By then I was eight, and for the first time in my life, I started school in Jakarta—basic education amid the chaos. We scraped by for about a year there, but stability was fleeting. In 1947 or so, the Red Cross stepped in and shipped my mom, dad (reunited post-internment), Louise, and me to the Netherlands. It was a very difficult experience for the whole family—culture shock, cold weather, rebuilding from scratch. The adjustment lasted a full two years, from ages 8 to 10, under my strict father's rule, who pushed discipline hard after all we'd lost.

Things seemed safer back in Indonesia by 1949, so my dad decided to return for his Goodyear work. We all went back to Jakarta, hoping for normalcy. But peace didn't last; the independence struggles boiled over into targeted attacks on Dutch people—kidnappings, shootings, outright killings in the streets. It became too dangerous. Around 1950, when I was about 12, Dad sent my mother, Louise, me, and our newly arrived baby brother back to Holland while he stayed behind, risking it all to try and salvage his company. We resettled in the Netherlands for good this time, and that's where I really grew up. School was rigorous, my father even stricter, but I threw myself into sports: soccer was my first love, then field hockey. At 13, in 1951 or 1952, a friend took me to a group workout session, and that's how I was introduced to tennis. I fell for it hard, but we could only play about six months a year outdoors—no indoor courts in those days—so winters meant ice skating or other games to stay fit.

* * *

In 1960, when I was 21, my parents decided to immigrate to the United States for better opportunities, landing us in San Diego, California. What a revelation—sunny skies, year-round tennis courts! Getting there was a great experience, though navigating this foreign country felt overwhelming at first. I played some local tennis, figuring things out. In 1962, I entered a tournament on a whim, beat the number 1 player from Pepperdine University, and just like that, I was offered a full scholarship. I enrolled at Pepperdine, played No. 1 singles and doubles, and earned All-American honors. Tennis came naturally with the consistent practice, but I left without graduating in 1964 to chase real-world paths.

Post-college, I tried odd jobs—sold encyclopedias door-to-door for a bit, but got fired quick for tracking dirt into a customer's pristine home. Needed something steadier. In 1967, at age 28, I started teaching tennis professionally at Morley Field, San Diego's public facility. That sparked everything. My coaching philosophy crystallized early: relentless repetition to groove groundstrokes—hard, fairly flat, penetrating shots hit low over the net, just 2 to 2.5 feet high. I called it the "Lansdorp Forehand" or "buggy whip forehand," rejecting the high-arcing "academy ball" topspin that I saw suiting college players but not true champions. I was a maverick—preferred one-on-one sessions in public parks over fancy academies, building accuracy, discipline, and mental toughness with drills like "20 at the baseline" (hitting 20 consecutive groundstrokes in bounds) or aiming at a tennis can perched on a broom handle. I'd roll out a supermarket cart full of balls for hour-long marathons, instilling fearlessness drawn from my own childhood survival.

In 1971, I replaced Vic Braden as head pro at the Jack Kramer Club in Rolling Hills Estates. That's where I truly put a club on the map as the birthplace of champions—it boomed under me for eight years, never before or after. Great stories from that era: I met Tracy Austin at age 7; she had raw talent, and I coached her to world No. 1, winning the 1979 US Open at 16—the youngest ever. Eliot Teltscher came at 10, developing that pure one-handed backhand. John Austin at 10 too. The

Fernandez girls—two sets of twins, including Anna-Maria Fernandez who climbed to No. 20 in the world. Trey Lewis, a standout with a great one-handed backhand. Non-members dropped in: Robert Van't Hof (who later became Davenport's traveling coach) and Brian Teacher, who reached No. 9 in the world en route to UCLA.

By the late 1970s and into the 1980s, I moved to the West End Tennis Club in Torrance. There, I worked with Pete Sampras starting at age 10, building his lethal running forehand that took him to No. 1 and multiple Slams. Lindsay Davenport from age 9—her dad had seen my work. Also Michael Joyce, Jeff Tarango, Derrick Rostagno, Stephanie Rehe, Melissa Gurney, the Basica brothers, Kimberly Po, Alexandra Stevenson, Justin Gimelstob. And my own daughter Stephanie—she became a great player herself, All-American at Arizona State University. I'm incredibly proud of her; she's following right in my footsteps, doing a fantastic job coaching now at West End. Go Steph!

In the 1990s, I joined the Riviera Tennis Club. That's when Maria Sharapova entered the picture in 1997 or so—she was 10, almost 11. Her dad Yuri had watched Davenport at the US Open (I was there coaching), and he wanted Maria to hit like her: those hard, flat, penetrating strokes. He had IMG call me, and our eight-year relationship kicked off. Yuri was sharp and dedicated; soon Maria mirrored Lindsay's groundies perfectly. That's the way to play on big stages!

I became one of the first non-family traveling coaches on the women's tour, logging miles and instilling that resilience. Overall, I coached four players to world No. 1—Tracy, Pete, Lindsay, Maria—who won 24 Grand Slams combined. Developed over 20 top-20 pros and 50 top-100 players, including Eugenie Bouchard, Julia Boserup, Anastasia Myskina, and more. My gruff, intimidating style—I'm 6'3", with a no-nonsense bark—built respect and lifelong bonds. Pupils like Tracy called me the best groundstroke teacher ever; Eliot Teltscher said my influence extended far beyond the court.

* * *

Outspoken as I was, I criticized modern shifts: the USTA's 2012 "10 and under" program with miniature courts and green-dot balls—unsuitable for real talents, I argued. Slammed Patrick McEnroe's player development too. In 2004, I joked that Sharapova, then a millionaire, owed me a Mercedes for never getting gifts from my star pupils.

The freeway commutes eventually wore me down, so I shifted to a public facility in the South Bay for a while. About seven years before 2012—around 2005—I went through a divorce after health scares, including a near-fatal infection that sidelined me. After recovering, my friend Joe Guarrasi offered me his private court in Palos Verdes. I've been there ever since, teaching into my 80s, loving the setup—no desire to go anywhere else.

Achievements piled up: USTA Lifetime Achievement Award in 2005, ITF Services to the Game Award, induction into the Southern California Tennis Hall of Fame in 2009, and as a Team USA Coaching Legend in 2013 alongside Nick Bollettieri and others. Never ran my own academy—stayed true to private, personal coaching.

In my later years, health declined, but I kept going. In July 2024, former players honored me at the Jack Kramer Club amid the downturn. I passed away on September 16, 2024, at age 85 in a West Carson, California, nursing facility from cardiopulmonary arrest, as my daughter Stephanie confirmed. Survived by her, I left a legacy: emphasizing discipline over raw talent, producing champions, and reshaping tennis technique and mindset forever.

The editor feels an obligation to explain Robert, but does not accept the responsibility to defend or agree with everything he said and did. If you learn one lesson from the master coach, Lansdorp, it would be to think for yourself and be adaptable. Some of what Robert says doesn't add up, is self-contradictory, and he could be unwilling to reconcile with other modes of tennis teaching. He might adopt aspects of other coaches teaching product, but then pan the orininal source. To Robert, there was HIS way. He acknowledged that there were other ways, but there was no negotiating the way when you were coached by him, except, ironically, that he wanted each player to figure out their way on their own. You might not like the words he used or the sarcasm he was famous for, but as you can see from the deep relationships he had with his players, he was a famously loving man. This editor saw firsthand the lovable teddy bear, hidden behind the hard shell exterior. Visiting Robert's Long Beach house, this editor was struck by the pictures on the wall, especially of candid shots between Robert and Maria Sharapova, whom he obviously loved like a daughter. Justin Gimelstob speaks of actually moving in to live with Robert while being coached by him. The Gimelstob family chose Robert because they were influenced by the Bobby Knight regime of basketball coaches and saw that most tennis coaches were perceived as less assertive. Justin has also been an outspoken and controversial figure in his own life, right or wrong, victim of media bias or not.

Robert's story includes being poisoned by those whose job it was to care for him, and being fed dubious food by the housemaid was part of the conflict in Indonesia during his childhood. To understand Robert and accept him a bit more easily with some grace, it's essential to know the formative trauma that he faced as his father was captured in a Japanese internment camp. For those reasons, take what you need, fill in the gaps, and leave the rest.

* * *

In the final stages of preparing this for publication, some friends at Patron's Coffee Shop in San Diego, asked about this work, which reminded the editor of this story: Robert got a lovely gleam in his eye as he shared that he was invited to speak at a tennis coaches' conference. He was teaching about how using an extreme downward angle with a western grip and a massive windshield wiper stroke would produce the maximum amount of topspin. The way he demonstrated it made it seem impossible for the ball to go over the net. After 20 minutes of explaining and demonstrating, but not hitting a ball, one coach raised his hand. "Robert, with all due respect, I know your resume, but I can't understand how that will work at that angle", the coach timidly asked probing question. Robert raised his arms, "Finally! I was waiting for someone to understand that it's not possible, but these are the kinds of things I hear you all teaching. What about the rest of you? You were going to sit there and listen to something you didn't understand, or was clearly wrong, but you weren't going to ask a question?" That was the effect of what he said, but it's been a few years since hearing that story. Maybe one of you were there, and if so and can tell the story better, please write and tell exactly how that went. Bottom line: Robert thought for himself, was adaptable, and wants you to think for yourself, that's Robert's greatest contribution to the world!

Other books by Bill Patton

Visual Training for Tennis

Entrenemiento Visual Para El Tenis

The Art Of Coaching High School Tennis + Workbook

Tennis Strategy 101

Net Gains: How to...

Tennis Strategy 201

Play Sports Right: Your Way! (Ages 8-13)

The Athlete Centered Coach

www.ingramcontent.com/pod-product-compliance
Lightning Source LLC
LaVergne TN
LVHW020937090426
835512LV00020B/3396